LONG ROAD
TO HARD TRUTH

LONG ROAD TO HARD TRUTH

THE 100-YEAR MISSION TO CREATE THE NATIONAL MUSEUM OF AFRICAN AMERICAN HISTORY AND CULTURE

Robert L. Wilkins

Printed in the United States of America by Proud Legacy Publishing

ISBN: 978-0-9979104-0-7 (hardcover)
ISBN: 978-0-9979104-1-4 (paperback)

Library of Congress Control Number: 2016950268

Book design by Daniel Kohan, Sensical Design & Communication

10 9 8 7 6 5 4 3 2

To Amina; as Stevie says, I'll be loving you always

And in memory of the millions of people of African descent who have passed from this Earth, without proper acknowledgement of their sacrifices for, and contributions to, the United States of America

CONTENTS

★

ACKNOWLEDGMENTS

★

The research and writing for this book has been nearly 20 years in the making, so I know that I have forgotten some who helped me along the way. To those of you, I apologize. Please charge it to my head and not my heart.

When I first began this journey, most of my time was spent in the Library of Congress, the National Archives, and the Moorland-Spingarn Research Center of the Howard University Library. The staff members at those three institutions were absolutely magnificent. I also benefited greatly from the assistance of the Hampton University Archives, the archives of the Commission of Fine Arts and the National Capital Planning Commission, and the presidential libraries of Presidents Coolidge, Hoover and Roosevelt. My colleague, Brett Kavanaugh, and my court's librarian, Patricia Michalowskij, graciously helped me track down sources. Alexis Anderson helped me research the early stages of the museum movement during her internship. My cousin Craig Wilkins also provided valuable feedback and research assistance. Many provided vital moral support in the early stages of my research, including my cousin Norman Scott El-Amin, my former church family at Union Temple Baptist Church, and my former colleagues at the Public Defender Service for the District of Columbia and at Venable LLP. Djakarta Jacobs, Tammy Boyd, LaRochelle Young, Donnice Turner, Kerri Watson, Tom Downs and Ron Christie provided critical insight to the behind the scenes activity within the commission staff, on Capitol Hill and in the White House, and these reflections helped round out the later chapters of the book.

When I first began writing in earnest, Conrad Rippy, my dear friend and former agent, imparted valuable guidance, and Susanna Margolis greatly helped with organizing my thoughts and drafting a marketing plan. Many people gave me great advice on the book writing and publishing process, including Ken Mack and Peter Slevin. My former law clerk, Clair Tzeng, provided critical writing and editorial assistance for the beginning chapters, and

Savannah Frierson also helped with editing the first half of the book. I could not have gotten all of the writing finished without the able drafting assistance of Brenda Windberg and the expert editing of her business partner, Lorin Oberweger. An army of my former law clerks provided invaluable editing, cite checking, and proofreading help, including Michael Shenkman, Julie Dona, Leon Kenworthy, Justin Baxenberg, Cyril Djoukeng, Richard Caplan, Matthew Sharbaugh, Calvin Nelson and Moxila Upadhyaya. I will be forever grateful to Delores Simmons and Michal Belayneh for helping to keep me organized and on track these past five years.

As described in these pages, I would not have been able to devote myself to this project without the tremendous support and sacrifice of my wonderful wife, Amina. She, and of course, our sons, Bakari and Alim, my mother, Joyce Wilkins, and my brother, Larry Wilkins, provided the inspiration to keep me going whenever I felt like giving up.

Last, and certainly not least, I thank God. In the words of Marvin Sapp, without Him, I "never would have made it."

PROLOGUE

★

WHY THIS BOOK?

Lewis Fraction was proud and confident, with a personality that could fill a room. He was a wise, God-fearing man who helped to mentor coming-of-age boys in our church youth program. He was also highly skilled in the fine art of trash-talking. Once, during a rap session about a man's duty to protect his home and family, he proclaimed that he could beat down *any* man who broke into his house and threatened his family—even Mike Tyson. "No man can take me in my own house," he said, because his will to protect his family and defend his home would help him overpower any threat. A bold statement indeed, especially for a man in late middle-age.

Perhaps no man could take him, but God could. In 1996, a few short years after that memorable proclamation, Brother Fraction was called from labor to rest. I respected him and had enjoyed getting to know him at our church activities, so my wife Amina and I went to his home to share our sympathies with his family.

It was a glorious evening. I sat there for hours, stuffing my face with delicious, down-home Southern food brought in by the deaconry, and listening. Many of the elders had gathered, and they were telling stories. All sorts of stories. Stories about growing up in the rural south or growing up in the city. About the myriad joys of youth—the courtship rituals, old dance steps, swooning over Sam Cooke, and marveling over the landing of the "Mothership" at a Parliament Funkadelic concert. There were also stories about all-Black, one-room ramshackle schoolhouses, and the nurturing but stern teachers who presided over the classrooms. Some of the elders remarked that they never saw a whole piece of chalk or a new textbook when they were growing up because their schools only ever got the worn, broken bits of chalk and beaten-up books that were the leftovers from the White schools. There were stories about countless indignities, both major and minor, and the psychological wounds they inflicted. There were stories of sit-ins, marches, and arrests. Stories that provoked laughter, tears, anger, and spirited debate.

Magnificent stories. Awful stories. Profound stories.

As we drove home that evening, I said to Amina, "why don't we have a museum to tell all of those stories?"

That's how this all began for me: with what seemed like a simple question. As I began to look deeper, I became committed—*obsessed*—with finding the answer.

The question was a complicated one, its answer even more so.

But nothing shook my belief that these stories deserved a home. Indeed, a prominent home. I also knew deep in my bones that the home should be in the nation's capital.

This was the crucible time for my devotion to the idea of a museum to commemorate Black history, its culture and stories, but my interest dated back much further. In 1987, I had been the Black History Month chair of our organization of African American law students. Our motto, emblazoned in black lettering on gold t-shirts, declared that, "every month is Black History Month." We organized a play, a concert, and other events on campus. It was loads of fun, and I became enamored with the importance of preserving and celebrating African American history and culture. I don't remember it, but I'm told that I talked about creating a national Black history museum during my interview for a job with the D.C. Public Defender Service in 1989.

Although any earlier talk may have been just that, talk, by 1996 I was serious. Since graduating from Harvard Law School, I had spent six years on the front lines of the criminal justice system as a public defender. I had seen far too many tragic stories of failed families and squandered opportunities.

When I started on the job, the nation was still in the middle of the crack epidemic, and Washington, D.C., was in the midst of a homicide epidemic. Indeed, the city that should have shone brightly as the nation's capital was infamous, instead, for being the "murder capital of the world." I had seen, up close and personal, too many gunshot wounds, patches where eyeballs used to be, autopsy reports, and bloody crime scene photos. I had visited far too many victims in hospital beds, clients in jail cells, family members in crappy little apartments, and witnesses on dangerous street corners. I still vividly remember being out with another lawyer looking for a witness in the middle of the afternoon, in broad daylight, when a dilapidated station wagon came slowly down the street toward us. There were four or five guys inside. The front passenger held an AK-47 rifle pointed upward but clearly at the ready. We tried to remain calm, and the car drove past without incident.

Back then, folks called those "war wagons."

But I was weary of the war. I was weary of the despair. I was weary of the seemingly never-ending negative news stories about the Black community. My clients and their broken lives were emblematic of those stories. Indeed, an eight-part series in the *Washington Post* about one of my clients, along with his mother and grandmother, won the 1995 Pulitzer Prize for Leon Dash as an epic "profile of a District of Columbia family's struggle with destructive cycles of poverty, illiteracy, crime and drug abuse."[1] I wanted to be a part of something positive. I wanted to *create* something. I wanted to help build a museum, so that those wonderful, painful, and profound stories that I heard all the time, not just in memory of Brother Fraction on that fateful evening, would finally have a home.

In my mind, those stories could serve a broader purpose. As a public defender, I represented kids who routinely skipped school and found themselves in trouble with the law. I wanted those kids to have a place where they could learn about the brave children of prior generations who were threatened, cursed, and spat upon as they sought to attend better schools. Perhaps a visit to the museum could show those kids why they should value the books, teachers, and educational opportunities that they had.

My clients were overwhelmingly African American, and so many of them, young and old, were devoid of genuine hope or self-esteem. I wanted them to have a place where they could see and hear the countless stories of how African Americans with seemingly little hope and even fewer resources were able to fight for freedom, seek justice, and change laws and attitudes. How, against all odds, African Americans won their freedom from slavery and their right to vote. I wanted them to have a place where they could see all of the contributions that African Americans have made to the United States, through service in the military, scientific inventions, and innovations in music and the fine arts. I wanted a place where poor Black people could go and see that they should have some hope, to see that they have the potential to do anything with their lives.

And after seeing so much racial division throughout my life, those stories could serve another important purpose: Unity. While working on this project with Sam Brownback, then Senator of Kansas, I heard him say that,

"America needs to lance the boil in this country that is race," and that a national museum in Washington could help move us in that direction. The stories about the fights for abolition and for civil rights are stories of unity; they are stories of people of all races, income levels, and ages coming together in pursuit of the equality and justice found in the Declaration of Independence and the Constitution. This could be a place where we have the much-needed and long-overdue national conversation on race that will help us to understand each other and come together.

In 1916, a group of African American leaders organized a not-for-profit corporation that would endeavor to construct a "National Memorial Building" dedicated "as a tribute to the Negro's contribution to the achievements of America." They had the same mission as I did: to tell these stories. So, I picked up the mantle they set down and, along with many others, carried on with it.

The journey of those brave and visionary souls, and of the many more who would come together over the next one hundred years to bring the dream of this museum into reality in the face of many obstacles, is a story that deserves recognition and remembrance. It is also a story that deserves a home.

That home is *Long Road to Hard Truth*.

CHAPTER ONE

★

THE GRAND OMISSION

In the days before radio, television, and the Internet, wondrous parades of marching troops called military reviews presented spectacles unlike any other. These reviews provided much more than entertainment. They served as symbols of strength, valor, and purpose, and provided a way for the civilian public to not only thank the soldiers, but affirm the worthiness of these soldiers' mission.

Because of its long tradition and storied role in the public consciousness, the call for a military review after four long, bloody years of conflict rang throughout the nation upon the Union's victory over the Confederacy in the American Civil War. In fact, the *Army and Navy Journal*, a weekly newspaper that closely covered all aspects of the war, expressed:

> [H]ope that by some ceremony a formal expression of the gratitude of the country may be conveyed to its defenders. We trust that a magnificent Review may reveal to the troops themselves and to the people, some idea of the great strength, the fine material, and the superb condition of their Army.[1]

The *New York Times* predicted such a review of the troops, "will be the greatest event of its kind…and its moral significance, as the closing scene in the drama, will be very striking."[2] Affirming the moral significance of the war was important as the Union's victory came at great cost to the nation. The conflict claimed the lives of more than 600,000 men in the Union and Confederate armies, and approximately one out of every fifty persons living in the United States had perished. Even the president of the United States,

Abraham Lincoln, fell victim, assassinated on Good Friday in 1865 by John Wilkes Booth. It would have indeed been passing strange for Union soldiers simply to muster out and go back to their homes without a fitting coda after so much loss and the almost complete destruction of the Republic. As David Blight, a prominent Civil War historian, insisted, "death on such a scale demanded meaning."[3]

Washington, D.C., became electric. The preparations for the Grand Review were so extensive and massive that they interrupted the most important legal proceeding in the nation: the trial of the eight conspirators in President Lincoln's assassination, which had been underway before a military commission in the Old Arsenal Building. The military commission thus deemed it appropriate to suspend the trial for those two days. In fact, all branches of government and public businesses were closed due to the Grand Review.

Tens of thousands of people crowded the sidewalks, balconies, windows, and rooftops to get a view of the soldiers who would march from the Capitol to the White House. Schoolchildren lined the parade route, cheering the soldiers and singing patriotic songs. Young ladies bestowed flowers and kerchiefs upon the heroic men. Banners hung from buildings all over the city, displaying patriotic and thankful messages on behalf of organizations, cities, and states from near and far. Reviewing stands were also set up in front of the White House and decorated with flags, stars, and flowers for President Andrew Johnson, cabinet members, General Ulysses S. Grant, the diplomatic corps, and various other dignitaries to view the parade. Even Secretary of State William H. Seward, still recovering from the grave wounds he had suffered during the attempt on his life carried out on the same night as Lincoln's assassination, attended the ceremonies.

Around 200,000 soldiers marched over the course of two days, with every colossal assemblage of troops requiring six hours to proceed in formation down Washington, D.C.'s main boulevard. Bands played while crowds cheered, saluted, and tossed flowers as each column of men passed through the throngs of humanity. Newspapers speculated that if these men had marched in single file, the line would have reached all the way to Richmond, Virginia, the erstwhile capital of the Confederacy.

As one popular publication stated, "[T]hey deserved an ovation of no ordinary character, and they received such a one as will forever remain green in their memories."[4] The event was declared a "splendid pageant,"[5] the "grandest spectacle of the age,"[6] and just about any other superlative one could imagine. The Grand Review truly had lived up to its name.

Or had it?

Rather than being represented in the Review as gallant, fighting soldiers, Blacks were shown as road-building auxiliary troops who supported the intrepid White soldiers, or as subservient and grateful former slaves who had been rescued by those White soldiers. In fact, out of those many thousands of soldiers, not a single member of the United States Colored Troops (USCT) made an appearance during those two celebratory days. The only African American presence consisted of a smattering of individuals who had accompanied Sherman's army, and none had engaged in combat.

These Black Soldiers on display in the Grand Review were not only meant to be subservient but to provide comic relief. Newspaper stories crowed with stories of the crowds ridiculing the Black soldiers, such as, "[T]wo Black soldiers of the largest size, riding very small mules, their feet nearly touching the ground, was regarded as a comic scene in connection with this part of the display, and occasioned general laughter."[7] There are numerous other accounts of sneers heaped upon the colored "pickaninnies," vagabonds, and "negroes blacker than Erebus" scattered among the gallantry.[8]

While most newspapers gave fawning coverage of the event without any mention of the missing colored combat troops, their absence did not go unnoticed. General Benjamin Butler, who had commanded USCT regiments during the war, gave a speech in his native Massachusetts decrying the omission, asking, "What shall we say of those colored men who [served] with instinctive loyalty and patriotism...shall he be denied even the poor honor of participating in the review of the troops who won those great victories, at the national capital?"[9] The Emancipation League passed a resolution at its annual meeting in Boston declaring the snub "insulting" to the colored troops and a shameful act of deference by the Union leadership to the rebels' hurt feelings.[10]

Many questioned how, and why, such an oversight could have occurred. Several newspapers recounted the exculpatory explanations of unnamed Union officials: that the omission was merely coincidence, as all of the USCT regiments were being deployed to locations in the West and the South and were therefore unavailable to participate in the event. Thus, the story went:

> There were no colored soldiers at that time nearer Washington than City Point (Virginia) where one or two brigades were stationed. It was contemplated by the Secretary of War and General Grant to order them to Washington for the sake of having them make part of the review...but it was finally

decided otherwise on the ground that it would occasion great trouble and expense, as other troops would have to be brought from other points to put in their place.[11]

This explanation was rather weak, given that some of those USCT deployments surely could have been delayed or adjusted. The official line became more implausible when one considered the 24th Regiment of the USCT was stationed right across the Potomac River at Camp Casey in Arlington, Virginia, on the very day the Grand Review had begun.[12]

Most of the press accepted the official explanation, and they exercised editorial privilege to criticize the "overzealous friends of the colored race" for making the "silly" suggestion the colored troops were left out of the procession.

Even famed abolitionist William Lloyd Garrison joined the many others willing to give the Union leadership the benefit of the doubt, proclaiming, "Our generals are more just than to refuse due honor to any soldier, white or black, who has battled nobly for the cause of the Union."[13]

Regardless if the exclusion of the colored troops from the Grand Review was intentional or coincidental, many African Americans felt the omission demanded remedy. So saying, a committee of Black citizens in Pennsylvania organized a reception for the colored troops in the state capital of Harrisburg.[14] Hundreds of soldiers from USCT regiments and detachments from various states came to participate in the festivities, and several thousand joyous and thankful Black residents cheered the marching soldiers and accompanied them on the procession through the city.

The parade paused at the mansion of former U.S. Senator and former Secretary of War Simon Cameron to receive his gracious remarks.

> I never doubted that the people of African descent would play a great part in the struggle, and am proud to say that all my anticipation has been more than realized. Your services, offered in the early part of the war, were refused, but when the struggle became of life and death, then the country gladly received you, and, thank God, you nobly redeemed all you promised. Like all other men, you have your destinies in your own hands, and if you continue to conduct yourselves hereafter as you have done in the struggle, you will have all the rights you ask for—all the rights that belong to human beings.[15]

And that, indeed, was the burning question: what would be the rights of the freedmen now that the war was over?

The Christian Recorder, the official newspaper of the African Methodist Episcopal (AME) Church and considered by many as the voice of Black America, undoubtedly spoke for countless freedmen when it demanded equal rights, including voting rights. In its view, the USCT had earned suffrage for the colored race, asking the nation, "Would you be guilty of depriving a race of people of the inestimable right of franchise and equality before the law, who, when the country was tottering under the throes of revolution and secession, and the terrible wings of eternal dissolution were hovering over her crushed and shattered institutions, shouldered the musket, and went bravely forward, in the face of all the contumely and prejudice which surrounded them and rescued the bleeding country from the murderous grasp of a power which the White man was unable to overcome?"[16]

These postwar declarations were unsurprising because many African Americans had long believed fighting in the Civil War would pave a path to full citizenship for all members of the colored race. As Frederick Douglass asserted in a famous speech to recruit Black men to join the USCT:

> Once let the Black man get upon his person the brass letters U.S., let him get an eagle on his button, and a musket on his shoulder, and bullets in his pocket, and there is no power on earth or under the earth which can deny that he has earned the right of citizenship in the United States.[17]

USCT regiments took this message to heart, as manifested by the motto on the flag of the 24th Regiment, "Let Soldiers in War Be Citizens in Peace!"

The colored troops knew why they went to war. They were not just fighting to end slavery; they were also fighting to become full citizens. But instead of being allowed to carry that battle flag, and its message, in the Grand Review, the 24th Regiment had been kept away from the Capitol and the White House—just the other side of the river but a world apart.

Another reminder of the gulf between Black and White Union soldiers appeared in newspapers on May 23, 1865, the first day of the Grand Review. The *New York Times* reported an "account of Negro revenge for the Fort Pillow massacre in Memphis." The story said that "the influx of poor old rebel troops into Memphis has caused a great excitement among the Negro troops. They got up a plot to assassinate every rebel soldier in Memphis in revenge for the Fort pillow massacre." According to the newspaper, "the Negroes refused to obey the order [to return to the fort] and a fight forthwith ensued. After a sharp conflict, twenty of the Negroes were killed and wounded and driven back in confusion into the Fort."[18] Similar reports appeared in dozens of other publications around the country, both large and small.

The Fort Pillow Massacre was an atrocity that occurred in April 1864, when forces under the command of General Nathan Bedford Forrest, a slave trader who would later found the Ku Klux Klan, overtook Fort Pillow screaming "no quarter!" and proceeded to indiscriminately slaughter the occupants of the fort, including all of the Black soldiers who failed to escape.[19] A Joint Committee of Congress concluded that "men, women, and even children, wherever found, were deliberately shot down, beaten, and hacked with sabres; some of the children not more than ten years old were forced to stand up and face their murderers while being shot; the sick and the wounded were butchered without mercy, the rebels even entering the hospital building and dragging them out to be shot, or killing them as they lay there unable to offer the least resistance."[20] While there was much outrage among Black troops about Fort Pillow, the inflammatory story about revenge printed in the *New York Times* was nonetheless a hoax and, three days later, the Gray Lady reported that General Cadwallader C. Washburn, the commander of the Union fort at Memphis, called the report "false in every respect."[21] Many believed that the hoax was maliciously and deliberately spread to damage the reputation of the Black soldiers and to undermine the quest for the right of Black suffrage.[22] Whatever the motive, the fabricated story of insubordination and revenge by Black troops in Memphis stood in stark contrast to the multitude of news stories of disciplined gallantry by the White troops in the Grand Review.

Perhaps because of the controversy that stemmed from USCT's exclusion from the Grand Review in Washington; perhaps because of the attention garnered by what would become known as the USCT Grand Review in Harrisburg; or perhaps because of his own desire to acknowledge USCT's service, President Johnson arranged to receive the First Regiment of the District of Columbia USCT at the White House. This invitation was fitting because the First Regiment was the original body formed pursuant to War Department General Order No. 143, which created the Bureau of Colored Troops in May 1863. This formal action allowed African Americans to serve as regular combat soldiers in the Union Army rather than as volunteers.

Led by its chaplain, Reverend (and later Bishop) Henry McNeal Turner of the AME Church, the First Regiment had served honorably and contributed its fair share to the Union victory. The infantry regiment fought in several battles in Virginia in 1864, and it participated in the Campaign of the Carolinas alongside General Sherman's troops in March and April 1865.

It was even present for the surrender of General Johnston and his Confederate army shortly after Lee's surrender at Appomattox. Nevertheless, the First Regiment did not escape the hostility and indignities suffered by other colored regiments. They too had suffered racially motivated attacks, threats, and other hostilities from District of Columbia residents from the moment they had formed.[23]

But all of those indignities would be forgiven in October 1865 when the regiment gained an audience with the President of the United States, with all of the pomp and circumstance attendant to such an occasion. Washington, D.C.'s African American community was ecstatic that the First Regiment was coming home, and even more so because the President would greet the troops. Newspapers called the event remarkable and historic. A veritable feast was planned to honor the returning heroes. A lengthy parade accompanied the troops as they proceeded through the city to the White House grounds. The First Regiment marched in formation, presented their arms, and showed the rigor and discipline that had acquitted them so well in battle.

Following these exercises, President Johnson addressed the colored troops. His speech, already noteworthy because it was his first address to colored troops since the close of the war, was even more significant because it spoke to the burning question: What should be the rights and position of the colored race following the Union victory?

President Johnson, while thanking the troops for their service, delivered his verdict. The defeat of the Confederacy did not necessarily mean Black freedmen would become full, or even partial, citizens of the land of liberty. In fact, the majority of the speech was an exhortation for colored troops to attend to all of their many obligations now that the war was over and to forgive any prior transgressions. He maintained the freedmen needed to prove themselves worthy before they could be deemed full citizens, even though they had already served honorably and valiantly in the defense of the Union. He even issued a challenge:

> Will you now, when you have returned from the Army of the United States
> and taken the position of the citizen; when you have returned to the avoca-
> tions of peace, will you give evidence to the world that you are capable and
> competent to govern yourselves?...[F]reedom is not simply the privilege to
> live in idleness; liberty does not mean simply to resort to the low saloons
> and other places of disreputable character. Freedom and liberty do not mean
> that the people ought to live in licentiousness; but liberty means simply to

be industrious, to be virtuous, to be upright in all our dealings and relations with men…[24]

In President Johnson's opinion, the colored soldiers would be required to pass a character and fitness evaluation before they could become eligible for citizenship. "You must give evidence that you are competent for the rights that the government has guaranteed to you." Citizenship had to be earned.

The President had essentially notified these soldiers that they were now on some form of "citizenship probation." Unlike the White soldiers who had been feted and granted, according to the *Washington Evening Star*, "[the opportunity to] resign their power and pomp, and return to the avocations of civil life, to enjoy the peaceful fruits of their sacrifices and heroism,"[25] the First Regiment would not get the power, much pomp, or the peaceful fruits of their sacrifices—at least not immediately.

Nearly every newspaper in the country reported the President's speech to the First Regiment. Many of them reprinted the entirety of the address verbatim. Most of the Northern newspapers complimented the President on his speech, with the *Daily National Republican* newspaper noting he had provided "sound practical advice to the colored people."[26]

Others understandably took offense. The *National Anti-Slavery Standard* insisted Johnson's speech was not just to the First Regiment, for it would "reach…the ears of two hundred thousand colored troops who wear or have just laid off the national uniform."[27] The paper contrasted this speech, in which he spoke to the colored troops "like a pedagogue or a drill master," with a recent speech he gave to former Confederates, whom he "greeted…as brothers." It also highlighted the "supreme hypocrisy" of Johnson's "lecture about licentiousness" to the colored troops, considering the Black Codes enacted throughout the South prohibited African Americans to have well-paid jobs or even to marry. The paper expressed its disbelief in Johnson's words with scathing bluntness, "the inconceivable impertinence to talk to these colored soldiers of colonization […] the speech as a whole [was] discreditable to the President, and an insult to the four millions of loyal citizens whom it consigns to a political purgatory."[28]

Considering President Johnson's address, perhaps the omission of the colored regiments from the Grand Review was a metaphorical rebuke of their proclamation that they had earned the right to full citizenship through their service in combat.

Ultimately, President Johnson's address informed the colored troops *their* war was not truly over. While they had prevailed in the war against the

Confederate Army, the colored troops would still have to fight for an equal place in America. They would have to fight for the right of suffrage, to serve on a jury, to own property, and for other basic civil liberties. Still, as the Harrisburg Review had shown, those veterans were proud of their service to the nation, and they wanted their legacy to be recognized appropriately.

Who would remember their sacrifice, and how would it be remembered?

George Washington Williams, perhaps the most prolific African American historian of the nineteenth century, lamented:

> The deathless deeds of the White soldier's valor are not only embalmed in song and story, but are carved in marble and bronze. But nowhere in all this free land is there a monument to brave Negro soldiers, 36,847 of whom gave up their lives in the struggle for national existence. Even the appearance of the Negro soldier in the hundreds of histories of the war has always been incidental. These brave men have had no champion, no one to chronicle their record, teaming with interest and instinct with patriotism.[29]

Williams argued Congress should establish such a monument and suggested placing it in a park adjacent to Howard University's campus in Washington, D.C. In Williams's mind, "a government of a proud, patriotic, prosperous, and free people would make a magnificent investment by erecting at the capital of the nation a monument dedicated to its brave Black soldiers."[30] Williams was not alone. Around this same time, the Colored Soldiers and Sailors League, a Union veterans' organization founded immediately after the war, was also calling for a monument to the colored troops in Washington.[31]

Williams was not just talk. He drafted legislation to create the monument to colored troops and led the lobbying efforts to gain support. In December 1886, Massachusetts Senator George Frisbie Hoar rewarded Williams's efforts by introducing the bill to Congress. Williams's testimony before the Senate Library Committee helped the bill gain committee approval, and his advocacy helped secure the bill's passage by the full Senate. It languished in the House of Representatives, however, unable to get out of committee. Williams's bill never became law.[32]

During the Grand Review, a banner hung from the Capitol asserting, "the only national debt we can never repay is the debt we owe the victorious Union soldier."[33] George Washington Williams and others rightfully asked, what of the debt due the colored Union soldier?[34]

CHAPTER TWO

★

THE QUEST FOR HONOR
INSPIRES A PLAN

Unfortunately for African Americans, the country made little attempt in the fifty years following the Civil War to repay the debt owed to them for their service—whether in a soldier's uniform or in tattered clothing on sweltering plantations. Instead, America seemed to double down on its failings by accruing new insults to Black people every time a slight step toward progress was made. While a gradual shift toward equality was to be expected, what African Americans often faced varied between "inclusion" in name only or outright rejection and degradation not much different from what plagued them before that Great War.

As much as the United States Colored Troops' exclusion from the original Grand Review had been a serious affront to those who had valiantly served, its reenactment fifty years later by the Grand Army of the Republic (GAR), and the circumstances surrounding the event, added almost equal insult to the injury.

Formed the year after the end of the Civil War, the GAR was the preeminent organization of Union veterans. Black and White Union soldiers alike were allowed to participate in state and national encampment activities under its auspices. In September 1915, the GAR held its 49th National Encampment in Washington, DC, and this encampment coincided with the fiftieth anniversary of the Union's Civil War victory. The reenactment of the Grand Review promised to celebrate the milestone; and this time, Black soldiers who had fought for the Union would march alongside the White soldiers.

Despite its progressive veneer, however, the GAR was a segregated organization and prevailing attitudes toward race influenced its operations.

The GAR organized itself by state "departments," and each department had several posts. Although some posts had both Black and White members, integration was not socially acceptable in most localities. As one White GAR leader put it in 1891:

> [T]he inexorable law of this social condition is such that the White man who associates upon terms of social equality with the Black man is barred from all association with the people of the White race and practically excluded from the privilege of earning a livelihood. It points the finger of scorn and derision to the wife of his bosom and the children of his love.[1]

Whatever gains had been achieved during Reconstruction, the period between 1865 to 1877 when the country put its best-faith effort into including African Americans in its full democracy, had been reverted and further trampled with the advent of Redemption and its Black Codes and Jim Crow laws. Indeed, more aggressive and insidious declarations were overtaking the country.

The insidiousness was evident in 1915, because that was not only the fiftieth anniversary of the Civil War's end, but also the year of a watershed moment in cinematic and social history. That year, American director D.W. Griffith released *The Birth of a Nation*,[2] a cinematic adaptation of the novel *The Clansman, The Birth of a Nation* written by Thomas Dixon Jr.

The story follows two White families, one from the North and one from the South, who find themselves in South Carolina during Reconstruction. Although they fought on opposite sides during the Civil War, they now unite in their opposition to the freedmen. In the film, the formerly enslaved win a majority in the South Carolina state legislature and oppressively rule over the White Southern populace.[3] Essentially, *The Birth of a Nation* was a condemnation of Reconstruction and the progress the country was trying to make, a manifestation of a White nightmare where Black people had the same access to citizenship and opportunity as they did.

The film offers gross and insulting caricatures of Black people, featuring uncivilized Black legislators[4] and licentious, sexually violent Black men whose sole aim is to prey on innocent and unwilling White women. Enraged by the indignities the White population suffers at the hands of the newly "empowered" Black people, the film's protagonist forms the Ku Klux Klan (KKK) "in defense of the[] Aryan birthright."[5]

The Birth of a Nation concludes with a depiction of the next election. This time, the KKK is out in full force and successfully intimidates South

Carolina's African-American population into giving up its vote and staying home.[6] This is a victorious and happy ending for those sympathetic to the Confederacy and White supremacy, to the point a writer for the *Confederate Veteran* magazine gushed that the film showed how the KKK:

> [U]pheld the Southern people in their refusal to surrender to the demand of the Radical Congress that they submit to [N]egro domination. They fought until the last vestige of that domination had disappeared. They affected a revolution. They added an unwritten amendment to the Constitution of the United States. That amendment reads as follows: "The American nation shall forever have a White man's government."[7]

The Birth of a Nation assaulted the notion of a free and equal Black man having a presence in the United States, resting on the premise that Black people were at the root of all problems facing the country, that liberty and unity could not coexist if Black people had equal rights to White people.

Promotional material represented that "[t]he events of the war between the states and of reconstruction, pictured in 'The Birth of a Nation,' are matters of authentic history."[8] The film's purported basis in historical truth could not have been a more grievous injury to African Americans at the time, especially those who had sacrificed on behalf of the Union Army.

Griffith, the director, invited a group of newspaper editors to view the film in New York and promised to withdraw the film if they found any inaccuracies in it.[9] He even declared he would pay $1,000 to anyone who could find falsehoods in his film; many were found, but he never paid up.[10]

As expected, the film drew universal condemnation from African Americans, led by the National Association for the Advancement of Colored People (NAACP), which believed the film's "heroic" depiction of the Ku Klux Klan glorified and encouraged the lynching of Black men—the very epidemic that helped spur the founding of the civil rights organization in 1909.[11]

At the time, the Supreme Court had not yet ruled that films fell within the First Amendment's protection of freedom of expression, so the film could be banned by state and local censor boards and licensing regulations. The NAACP and other opponents of *The Birth of a Nation* sought, sometimes successfully, to ban it outright or have the most objectionable scenes cut as the film made its way across the country from theater to theater. Many protests of the film arose, and some turned violent. In Boston, riots erupted outside a theater after efforts to ban the film failed; in Philadelphia, rioting was so intense that it led to several deaths.[12]

Outside of protests, many African Americans decided to fight in less direct ways, chiefly to challenge the film's "truths" by promoting an accurate recounting of Black experiences. Most notably, famed historian Carter G. Woodson founded the Association for the Study of Negro Life and History (today called the Association for the Study of African American Life and History or ASALH) in 1915. Its primary objective was to counter attacks against the character of African Americans, including those perpetrated by *The Birth of a Nation*. Woodson went on to establish *The Journal of Negro History*, *The Encyclopedia Africana*, and the Negro History Week, which later became Black History Month.

The controversy surrounding *The Birth of a Nation* engulfed the capital shortly after its first private screening in Los Angeles, on February 8, 1915. As the NAACP and others strategized ways to use boycotts, protests, censor boards, and challenges to licenses and permits to stop the film's showings, the purveyors of the film planned their counterattack. Most notably, *Clansman* author Thomas Dixon Jr. persuaded President Woodrow Wilson, with whom he had attended Johns Hopkins University, to screen the film in the White House.[13] Washington newspapers informed the public of the upcoming White House screening of the then-relatively unknown film, saying the picture, "will show the progress of the colored race in this country from the days of slavery down to the present time," and that the President was interested in the film because of "the great lesson of peace it teaches."[14]

On the evening following the White House screening, the National Press Club hosted a private screening in a large ballroom of the Raleigh Hotel in Washington. Dozens of high-ranking government officials attended, including the Chief Justice, other members of the Supreme Court, Senators and Representatives.[15] Dixon and Griffith believed these private screenings to national leaders gave the filmmakers and theater owners ammunition for their later fights with the licensing and censoring authorities: if the film could be shown in the White House, how could it be inappropriate for viewing by the common citizen? Indeed, the filmmakers would go on to win more censorship battles than they lost, despite the fact President Wilson, facing political pressure, later released a public statement indicating he, "was entirely unaware of the character of the play before it was presented, and has at no time expressed his approbation of it."[16]

The specter of *The Birth of a Nation* lingered in Washington as the colored Union veterans arrived for the GAR National Encampment in the fall of 1915. Newspapers published stories about the film practically every day as protests and lawsuits gave the film free publicity and contributed to its record-breaking ticket sales.

Surely, Black veterans felt the sting of its presence, even as they sought out old brothers-in-arms and tried to celebrate their service to the nation. The Rev. Dr. James Shera Montgomery, a prominent minister who would later become Chaplain of the House of Representatives, even delivered a sermon entitled "Birth of a Nation" at a special service for the GAR members who had travelled to Washington for the Encampment.[17]

However, these Black veterans did not need a film to remind them of their second-class status while at the Encampment. The GAR was already doing so. In the months prior to the Encampment, the GAR had appointed a "Public Comfort Committee" to coordinate all arrangements for entertaining the Union veterans in Washington, and no Black member had been named to it. The *Washington Bee*, a Black newspaper, chastised the GAR for the exclusion, sarcastically noting, "It is to be regretted that this city doesn't have one representative colored citizen of sufficient intelligence to be appointed on the public comfort committee...."[18]

In the face of this exclusion, the Black community in Washington stepped up to the challenge of ensuring the heroic colored veterans would be properly hosted during the Encampment. They formed the Colored Citizens Committee for the Entertainment of the Veterans of the Encampment. The committee arranged transportation, lodging, banquets, tours, and other activities for the visiting Black veterans by raising money from churches, society groups, and other organizations.[19] People donated automobiles so veterans could take sightseeing tours of the city and opened up their homes so visiting veterans would have comfortable lodging, given their exclusion from the segregated hotels.[20] They also organized a concert and receptions. The committee extended a formal invitation to President Wilson to address them at a grand reception planned for the eve of the reunion march.[21] Unsurprisingly, he declined, choosing instead to attend the main reception sponsored by the GAR. As the nation's Commander in Chief, he received a warm reception from the assembled White veterans. In his address, President Wilson thanked them for their service and said he was "proud to be [their] servant." He explained that he loved this country not just because it was his home, but also because he saw this country "as a great instrument for the spirit of mankind." Wilson proclaimed to this group of Union veterans that:

> This nation was from the beginning a spiritual enterprise, and you have
> seen the spirits of the two once-divided sections of this country absolutely

united…[from] a war which seemed as if it had the seed of every kind of bitterness[…]it has seen a single generation put bitterness absolutely out of its heart, and you feel as I am sure the men who fought against you feel, that you were comrades even then, even though you did not know it, and that now you know that you are comrades in a common love for a country which you are equally eager to serve.

He celebrated this reconciliation as "a miracle of the spirit." Wilson, who was born shortly prior to the Civil War in Virginia, and raised in Georgia and South Carolina, even strangely proclaimed, "This is one of the very few wars in which in one sense everybody engaged may take pride."[22]

On the next day, approximately 20,000 veterans participated in the re-enactment of the Grand Review. Even though there was only one-tenth of the number of original participants, the diminished size did not result in diminished spirit. The veterans gathered at Peace Monument, which had been constructed to honor sailors lost at sea during the Civil War. From this location just west of the Capitol, they made the two-mile trek down Pennsylvania Avenue past the White House, where President Wilson and other national luminaries saluted them. Along the way, more than a quarter million people lined both sides of the Avenue to cheer the veterans. The former soldiers marched proudly, many struggling mightily with the aid of a cane or the shoulder of a stronger comrade. Several became exhausted and collapsed along the Avenue, as nurses and others ran to resuscitate them and tried to help them complete the trek from the Capitol to the White House so that they could salute the President. Several of the aging veterans collapsed with exhaustion as soon as they passed the presidential reviewing stand.[23] Those too weak or lame to attempt the journey on foot brought up the rear in scores of automobiles.

President Wilson's theme of reconciliation manifested itself during the parade as a handful of Confederate veterans in uniform joined the march and proceeded arm-in-arm with the Union veterans. These scenes led to uproarious applause and cheers from the crowd, who marveled at the happy reunion of blue and gray. Parade attendees observed no one seemed to enjoy those scenes more than President Wilson himself.[24]

The reunion was, however, surely bittersweet for Black veterans and the Black community that gathered to support them. While they were able to right the wrong of exclusion from the original Grand Review and celebrate the defeat of the Confederacy, now, they lived every day under Jim Crow.

As the *Afro-American Ledger* observed:

[N]otwithstanding the fact that they wore the uniform, and the badge of faithfulness, there was hardly a single place of entertainment, not kept by a member of their own race[,] that was opened to them. Not a single place of amusement in the city of Washington, the capital of the nation they gave their blood to defend, would have given them a decent seat....[25]

When Black citizens protested their exclusion from the Public Comfort Committee prior to the Encampment, GAR leadership responded that most states were planning activities for their native sons and therefore responded that "[i]t would be entirely proper for the 90,000 colored people of Washington to organize similarly and independently."[26] This explanation dodged the essential concern of racial segregation. The fact some states offered entertainment alternatives for their White veterans meant nothing to the visiting Black veterans from those states, who would have had no social activities to attend at all had it not been for Black Washingtonians organizing to provide them.

Fortunately, there was a boon to be had thanks to the GAR's exclusion and prevarication. The Committee of Colored Citizens decided to take the funds left over from their activities during the Grand Review's Fiftieth Anniversary and use them "as a nucleus for the erection of a monument in this city to the memory of the colored soldiers and sailors who fought in the wars of our country."[27] After the Encampment, the *Afro-American Ledger* asked, "[W]hat has these fifty years brought of fame or honor to them that they might feel proud that they once wore the uniform and fought for a grateful country?"[28] The question, echoing the concern George Washington Williams had expressed a generation earlier, finally had the start of an answer in the form of this proposed national monument.

But the complete answer would be a very long time coming.

CHAPTER THREE

★

FROM MEMORIAL TO MUSEUM

The 1916 proposal to build a memorial honoring Black soldiers and sailors was hardly without similar precedent. Just a few years prior, Congress had passed bills to appropriate funds for a monument commemorating the services and sacrifices of White women to the Union's cause during the Civil War, resulting in the construction of the American National Red Cross headquarters,[1] as well as a monument to commemorate the services and sacrifices of White women during the American Revolution, resulting in the construction of the headquarters for the Daughters of the American Revolution.[2] Viewed in this context, a memorial honoring African Americans who had fought in all past wars of the United States was a modest proposal. Nonetheless, it did not garner the same support as those memorials to White women.

The National Memorial Association (NMA) memorial proposal was, in essence, a counterattack to force Congress to acknowledge the contributions of Black soldiers past and present. The organization filed its official articles of incorporation with the city on March 9, 1916, and immediately started advocating its cause. At least six of the organization's twelve charter members had been officers on the Colored Citizens Committee, including Ferdinand Lee, who had served as the Committee's president and became the NMA's founding president.

As citizens were writing to the District of Columbia Board of Commissioners about the proposed ban on *The Birth of a Nation*, Lee wrote to the commissioners seeking their assistance in finding a site for the proposed monument. And just as they had done with respect to the film complaints, the commissioners pushed away Lee, saying they had no authority in the matter and directing him to consult with city planning officials instead.³

The NMA vigorously rallied support for its cause. Within two months of its launch, it organized a "patriotic platform meeting" at the 19th Street Baptist Church in Washington, even recruiting United States legislators to speak in support of the proposed monument. Flyers were passed out all over the city, urging people to attend the gathering, which would be held eleven days after Griffith's ignominious film ended its run. Emblazoned across the top of the flyer in all capital letters was the phrase "THE BIRTH OF A RACE," a reminder that the NMA intended not only to honor the service of colored soldiers and sailors, but also to counter the slander on the Black community in popular culture.⁴

One cannot overstate the ambition and audacity of the NMA's undertaking. Not only did members propose a monument to celebrate the accomplishments of Black soldiers amid the cultural war surrounding *The Birth of a Nation*, but they did so in the face of concerted congressional efforts to ban further African American enlistment in the military. On July 27, 1916, Congressman Thaddeus Caraway, Democrat of Arkansas, introduced bill H.R. 17183, explaining, "[W]hen you arm a Negro and especially when you vest him with federal authority, you bring out the evil that is in him. He becomes a dangerous, swaggering, terrorizing bully."⁵

In remarks delivered on the House floor, Caraway argued his bill should be passed in order to "confine enlistments to the best blood that ever flowed in human veins—the blood of the White race." Caraway proclaimed, "[T]he Negro is temperamentally unfit to wield authority," and, unlike the Union, the Confederacy had not armed Black soldiers even at its most desperate stage "because they knew the temperament and character of the Negro race, and they would not inject barbarism into civil strife."⁶ Caraway ended his speech by asserting White men of good character were refusing to join the military because they did not want to serve on equal footing with Black soldiers—especially the Navy, where "both White and Negro sailors serve aboard the same ship, eat in the same mess hall, and sleep in the same ward."⁷ Caraway received sustained applause at the conclusion of his remarks, but ultimately his bill did not pass. Nevertheless, it was reflective of the attitudes that prevailed among many in the country—and in Congress—when it came to the Black soldier.

While the NAACP had criticized Caraway's bill as another example of "the oppression and humiliation of colored American citizens,"⁸ the organization and Black Americans as a whole did have prominent government allies, including Secretary of War Newton Baker and Congressman Murray Hulbert, Democrat of New York. Hulbert noted the bravery and patriotism exhibited by Black soldiers and sailors throughout history and denounced "this intemperate and unpatriotic action upon the part of the representative who had the temerity to introduce such a measure."[9] Acknowledging the movement started by the NMA, Hulbert instead suggested Congress should support the effort to erect a memorial to the African American heroes who had served their country and sacrificed their lives in the armed forces.

Another strong congressional advocate for the NMA was Missouri Republican Leonidas Dyer, a military veteran who served in the Spanish American War. Dyer was an outspoken and steadfast supporter of causes that predominantly affected Black people and later became the author and biggest proponent of a federal bill to prohibit lynching.

On December 12, 1916, Dyer introduced HR 18721, the first of many bills inspired by the NMA to create a monument or memorial dedicated to Black soldiers and sailors. The bill proposed a $10,000 up-front appropriation to defray the cost of planning, designing, and constructing a memorial that would cost no more than $100,000. The bill also proposed forming an entity called the National Memorial Commission to supervise the effort. This latter proposal was quite extraordinary because the commission would be racially integrated.

Although based in Washington, the NMA sought to create a nationwide movement in support of the memorial. It worked with African American leaders around the country to have every governor appoint an official representative to the National Memorial Commission to be affiliated with the effort.

By May 1917, the organization had persuaded thirty-nine governors of the then forty-eight states to appoint such representatives to support the project. As national support grew, Congressman Dyer introduced more bills in 1917 to create the proposed memorial.

None of the bills introduced in 1917 received a committee hearing or a vote; a far more pressing event demanded the country's attention: World War I.

The United States entered World War I in 1917; and, as in every prior war, African Americans valiantly served their country. When peace returned, interest in a national memorial to Black soldiers and sailors remained high. Three more bills to create the memorial were introduced in 1919. In December 1919, thousands of people attended a NMA rally at the Liberty Hut in

Washington in support of the memorial. Ferdinand Lee presided over the gathering. The event raised several hundred dollars that evening, and more was pledged toward the effort.[10]

Speakers at the rally lauded Black military personnel in the nation's recent victory, extolling their bravery and sacrifices. Among the invited speakers was Colonel Charles Young, the third African American to graduate from West Point and the highest ranking African American officer in the United States Army at the time. Young had served bravely in World War I, and while he appreciated the enthusiasm and thanks expressed by the throngs, it was a bittersweet occasion. Rather than being greeted as equal citizens by a grateful nation, Young and other Black soldiers had returned home to face discrimination, segregation, and even lynching. Colonel Young undoubtedly represented many of them when he declined to speak at the Liberty Hut rally:

> He was opposed to a monument of bronze or stone in honor of the Negro soldier dead. But he did request of Congress a memorial to the Negro dead and that that memorial be the thing for which these Negros gave their lives—liberty, justice, equal opportunities in educational facilities, the suppression of lynching by making it a federal crime[, and] the abolition of Jim Crow Cars.[11]

Lynching, which entailed murder and terrorism, frequently involved merciless torturing of victims in a perverse carnival-like atmosphere. Surrounded by bloodthirsty spectators, victims were often beaten severely or disfigured by having their ears or fingers cut off, or their eyes gouged out of their sockets. Dismembered body parts were handed out to the crowd as souvenirs. Sometimes, victims were burned alive rather than hung from a tree or a post.[12]

Lynching deprived African Americans of their humanity and reinforced the belief they were less than human. Therefore, the monument to Black soldiers would be more than just about honoring them, but also about reminding the country of Black people's humanity as a whole. If the country could see and recognize all the contributions African Americans had made for the national common good, then surely the country could not be so callous in its inhumane and unjust treatment of them. Anti-lynching advocates, many of whom were members of the NMA, realized humanizing African Americans in the country's eyes was a key element in the fight. The National Equal Rights League sent an official petition to Congress, asking it to publish a document memorializing the contributions, loyalty, and service of Black people as a means to fight the existential threat caused by endemic racism in America:

> The colored race has not available the necessary means to systemically and comprehensively gather and publish the facts concerning their achievements in the United States as a world group and place them before the American people. That each member of the race feels keenly the handicap suffered thereby, and believes were a full, just, and widespread showing of these facts, narrating the part the race has borne toward building up America on land and sea, placed before the world, it would serve effectually to greatly modify feeling against the colored race and be of inestimable help to it in its battle for a man's chance in the struggle for existence.[13]

Colonel Young did not stand alone in demanding Congress pass federal anti-lynching legislation. Fighting lynching became a top priority for African Americans, including those who supported the NMA's proposed memorial.[14]

African American leaders understood that efforts to pressure Congress into passing anti-lynching legislation required flawless strategy to succeed given that there were members who openly defended lynching on the House floor. For instance, Congressman James Thomas Heflin, Democrat of Alabama, advised Republicans against proposals to integrate the races and explicitly condoned the extrajudicial killings of Black men accused of raping White women. He warned that Republicans were "sowing dragon's teeth in the path of White women wherever the Negro problem is present" and declared, "[W]hen a Negro commits the crime of rape on a White woman he must die." Heflin's comment received applause in the House chamber.[15]

Conversely, Congressman Dyer—the author of the first anti-lynching bill introduced in Congress and the idea's strongest proponent—believed highlighting the loyal service of Negro soldiers to the nation would strengthen the case for the federal anti-lynching law. In 1919, Dyer gave several lengthy speeches on the House floor, painstakingly describing the heroic acts of Black soldiers during World War I. In doing so, Dyer hoped:

> [O]ut of this war and the sacrifice made by the colored people that there will come a wave throughout the land of patriotic fervor on the part of all of the people that will demand of those charged with the responsibility of

government that the colored people shall receive and that they will have their rights as citizens protected. There ought not to be any need for these people and their White friends petitioning the Congress of the United States that laws be enacted to give them justice.[16]

Dyer's bill to prosecute lynching on the federal level would not pass through Congress for years, but he continued introducing anti-lynching legislation during every session in which he served and vowed to do so until such a law was enacted. As he later put it, lynching was an abomination to the fundamental principles of Christianity and democracy, declaring, "We must recognize the Negro as a man, a human being."[17]

The push for a memorial became inextricably linked to the advocacy supporting anti-lynching legislation and other anti-discrimination bills. The growing scale of the NMA's proposal over the years reflected this greater mission to humanize a race that had heretofore been marginalized and subjected to public hatred and ridicule.

By the early 1920s, NMA expanded the scope of the project beyond the proposed construction of a towering shaft or statue to that of a "memorial building," a place to recognize the Negro as a fellow human being who has contributed greatly to the nation. The building would not only commemorate Negro soldiers and sailors, but also Negro achievement in business, education, politics, the arts, and every other aspect of American life. It would be equipped with:

> [A]n auditorium ample to house some 3,000 or 4,000 people...a hall of fame, art and music rooms, library and reading rooms, museum, statues and tablets, which are proposed to commemorate the deeds American Negros wrought for the perpetuation and advancement of the nation, which would embody the utilitarian, aesthetic, and reverential, thus meeting the monument building ideas of the age as well as serving the race in a useful way.[18]

Anticipated expenses grew along with the memorial's scope. The initial bills introduced in 1916 and 1917 had assured the National Memorial Commission would raise an amount not to exceed $100,000. By 1919 and 1924, the legislation provided a budget to not exceed $500,000; by 1927, the bill stated the budget would be not less than $500,000. These later bills also requested an up-front appropriation of $50,000 as seed capital for the National Memorial Commission to hire staff, support administrative efforts, and procure a building site.

But securing the necessary funding for the expanded project was not the only hurdle facing the NMA and its supporters. The proponents of the memorial building continued to confront racist attitudes in Congress, including the belief that Black people best served the nation when they remained loyal servants to their "White masters."

The United Daughters of the Confederacy (UDC) and its supporters employed the same tactic as the NMA, to humanize African Americans, but with far a different narrative. The UDC, an organization that grew out of various women's groups providing support to the Confederate soldiers during the Civil War, urged Capitol Hill lawmakers from 1922 to 1924 to introduce bills authorizing a "monument in memory of the faithful colored mammies of the South" in the nation's capital.[19] Greatly offended by a memorial solely focused on the nostalgia of the faithful of Black housekeeper who nursed the slave master's children, the African American community offered considerable opposition.[20]

Despite the opposition, a "Mammy Memorial" bill sponsored by Senator John Sharp Williams, Democrat of Mississippi, passed the Senate in 1923;[21] however, the bill died in the House and thus never became law. Even though the UDC's vision for the colored mammy memorial was never realized, the impassioned fight for and against it was emblematic of the battle over the American narrative and memory, much like the controversy over *The Birth of a Nation*. It was another reminder of what was at stake for the National Memorial Association.[22]

Unlike the Mammy Memorial, the NMA was not able to convince either chamber of Congress to pass any of its bills, despite hearings in the House Committee on the Library in 1919 and 1924. But the tide began to turn in 1928, when the Committee on Public Buildings and Grounds, chaired by Richard Elliott of Indiana, held a hearing on House Joint Resolution 60, a bill that had been introduced that year by Congressman Will Taylor of Tennessee. The NMA's hard work to garner national support for the legislation was on full display at the hearing. Congressman Taylor and Ferdinand Lee read letters of support from individuals and organizations around the country. Lee also showed a photograph of the proposed building's model, which had been designed by African American architect Edward R. Williams, demonstrating the gravity and professionalism of the endeavor.

The most persuasive evidence in support of the legislation came from heartfelt testimony. Mary McLeod Bethune, founder of Bethune–Cookman College and president of the National Association of Colored Women, submitted that the memorial building "is merited by my race, for great has

been their contributions to the worthwhile accomplishments of our splendid country." She stressed that the memorial's construction would mean a
great deal "to the youth of the race who[se] hearts are filled with a desire
for service, [for] it will mean an inspiration and a beacon light, erected in
commemoration of what their people have meant to America's civilization
in the past."[23] Robert Lee Brokenburr, a prominent African American attorney in Indianapolis who represented entrepreneur and activist Madam
C. J. Walker,[24] wrote to remind Congress that achievements of the Negro
community never had been specifically highlighted:

> This idea of the insignificance of the Negro, which is contrary to fact, is so
> deeply rooted in the minds of most people that the large majority of students
> attending our public institutions of learning get no impression from the
> books used therein that Negros have made any worth-while contributions
> to American advancement and graduate with the false impression that this
> group of loyal patriots in peace and in war are more of a burden to America
> than an asset to it.[25]

Witnesses read editorials from the Black press into the record, including
one from the *Louisville News* reminding Congress that fair-minded White
people, as well as those indifferent to Black Americans, can be influenced
by "derogatory news" about Black people and never realize "our true worth
as individuals or as a group," arguing that the proposed memorial building
could change some of those attitudes.[26] Another editorial from the *Amsterdam News*, the veritable Harlem newspaper, advised Congress "this is the
greatest cultural project ever undertaken in behalf of the Negro," and urged
Congress to support the project because of African American contributions
in the military, unpaid slave labor, and "his music[, which] is being hailed as
American's only original contribution to the culture of the world."[27]

Ferdinand Lee reminded Congress that "no other race has advanced as
astonishingly with the period of fifty years as the Negro has done [since
the Civil War]," and the memorial building should be constructed as "evidence of actual and authentic recognition of a people who have complied
both theoretically and literally with American standards as fixed and practiced by White Americans."[28] Congressman Will Wood of Indiana noted
the positive impact of seeing exhibitions of African American art, inventions, and other achievements at the Atlanta Exposition a few years prior,
proclaiming, "[T]hese things are instructive. They are illustrative. They
are elevating. They demonstrate the fact that these people are doing for

themselves in spite of the handicap in which they were so long placed."[29]

Opponents to the bill were also present at the hearing. Most conspicuously, Congressman Charles Edwards of Georgia asked whether any other race or group had sought such a memorial, suggesting this was undue special treatment for Black people. In response, Congressman Maurice Thatcher of Kentucky stated, "if it should be said that no other race has had any consideration of this character, I would say in response to that suggestion that no other race has given 250 years of unrequited toil to America."[30]

Mary Church Terrell,[31] the first president of the National Association of Colored Women and a founding member of the NAACP, reminded the committee that even though Crispus Attucks, a Native Black man, was the first patriot to die in the Revolutionary War, "there is not a public building in the capital of the nation for which Crispus Attucks fought, in which his statue or that of any other hero of African descent may be placed."[32]

Some Congressmen raised questions about the cost of procuring a site and asked whether Congress should approve anything at all, given that so many costs were unknown. Congressman Edwards warned that the $50,000 appropriation would not be the last and there inevitably would be requests for more funds in the future. In response, Ferdinand Lee countered that the American Red Cross had sought and received additional funding to complete its memorial building.

In contrast to the contentious committee hearings in the House, the process in the Senate moved more smoothly, thanks to Senator Charles Curtis, Republican of Kansas, who supported the NMA. From his powerful position as majority leader, Senator Curtis shepherded the bill's passage with one important amendment: it allowed for the $50,000 in public funds to be provided only after at least $500,000 had been raised by private contributions to the National Memorial Commission. Senator Curtis' bill passed the Senate without debate or controversy.[33]

Following the committee hearing, the memorial building legislation was granted consideration before the full House of Representatives with just two days left in the session. Congressman Taylor expressed his disappointment at the prevalence of racial prejudice, chastising his colleagues:

[P]roud representatives of the great, stalwart, independent, and arrogant Caucasian race gainsaying and denying the small, paltry, insignificant modicum of consideration and encouragement to a people just a little more than half a century removed from penal servitude and a people who have contributed so much in a material and patriotic way to build up this great country and make it as it is today the envy and admiration of the nations of the earth."[34]

Rather than pushing his bill, which would have provided the $50,000 appropriation up front, Congressman Taylor asked the House to concur with the Senate version, which would send the bill to the president to be signed into law. Congressman Taylor reminded the House that the bill "will only cost the Federal Treasury the puny sum of $50,000.00," and those funds would not be made available until at least a half-million dollars had been raised.[35]

Congressman John E. Rankin, Democrat of Mississippi, was unimpressed, deriding the bill as merely "a political measure [...] intended to catch Negro votes." Rankin argued the bill was "an outrage" because no such bill should pass to favor the Negro race while there had yet to be a law providing for the creation of a memorial to Thomas Jefferson.[36]

Congressman Taylor challenged Rankin to introduce a bill to construct a Jefferson memorial and said he would cheerily support it. Rankin evaded the challenge, no doubt because his reason for opposing the legislation was not that it somehow slighted Jefferson, but rather that it gave credit and respect to African Americans.

Nevertheless, the bill's proponents fended off its opponents' delaying tactics and it passed by an overwhelming majority. President Coolidge signed the bill into law on the morning of March 4, 1929. It was his final day in office and one of his last official presidential acts.[37]

The bill to create a National Memorial Building to Negro Achievement and Contributions to America became law with literally not a moment to spare.

CHAPTER FOUR

★

DEATH AND INDIFFERENCE

While the passage of the bill to create the National Memorial Commission was widely celebrated in the press and the African American community, the sentiment was not unanimous.

One Black commentator characterized the bill's passage as "an empty honor" because the Commission would have to raise $500,000 before it could tap the $50,000 in public funds.[1] Mordecai W. Johnson, president of Howard University, and Nannie Helen Burroughs, president of the National Training School for Women and Girls, both declined appointments to the Commission because of their concerns about the lack of funding and the formidable fundraising challenge ahead.

Johnson observed, "The legislation creating the Commission does not place the members thereof in a position to perform effectively their defined functions."[2] But Ferdinand Lee, the dedicated president of the NMA, would not let these obstacles deter them from their goal.

Lee immediately began promoting the memorial building, visiting churches and encouraging their congregations to support the project[3]; he also wrote letters to newspapers, thanking their readers for supporting the legislation.

One month after the bill passed, Lee organized a victory celebration at the Metropolitan AME Church in Washington, complete with a musical program and addresses by local African American leaders and congressional sponsors of the bill. The invitees even included Matthew Henson, the African American member of Commander Robert Peary's expedition to the North Pole.[4] Lee also arranged for Edward R. Williams, the architect who had designed a model of the memorial building, to meet with Charles Moore, head of the powerful Commission on Fine Arts,[5] a newly created entity responsible for planning building projects in Washington, particularly those on the National Mall. Lee sought their input on plans for the building as well as the building's location.

On September 20, 1929, President Hoover appointed members of the National Memorial Commission. Several of the new commissioners were active with the NMA. In addition to Ferdinand Lee and Mary Church Terrell, appointees included John R. Hawkins,[6] who also served as the NMA's treasurer, and two of the association's vice presidents: Mary McLeod Bethune[7] and Reverend L.K. Williams.[8] The remaining seven commissioners, also prominent African Americans, were William Gaston Pearson,[9] Webster L. Porter,[10] Reverend J.R. Ransom,[11] Reverend H. Clay Weeden,[12] William C. Hueston,[13] Paul R. Williams,[14] and Matthew T. Whittico.[15]

The African American press reported extensively on the appointments, including coverage in the *Chicago Defender*, the *Philadelphia Tribune*, the *Topeka Plain Dealer*, and the *New York Amsterdam News*. Excitement surrounding the Commission grew even more when it was announced that President Hoover would meet with the commissioners at the White House. Taking advantage of the good press, the newly minted Commission mobilized the nationwide network established by the NMA by summoning to Washington the state commissioners appointed by their governors for a public meeting on the night after the White House visit.

Timing, however, could hardly have been worse for the National Memorial Commission.

Just a month after President Hoover's appointments, the United States suffered one of the most devastating financial setbacks in its history: the stock market crash of 1929. Investors lost billions of dollars on the New York Stock Exchange in October 1929, prompting a global economic meltdown of an unprecedented magnitude and the beginning of the Great Depression. The collapse of the American and worldwide economy was particularly distressing to the Commission, which was struggling to raise the funds necessary for its day-to-day operations.

Since Congress had stripped provisions in the legislation that would have granted the Commission an upfront appropriation to cover startup costs such as hiring staff and paying administrative expenditures, it was the Commission's sole responsibility to find ways to cover its most basic expenses. Hoping funds would be available to reimburse them later, commissioners paid for their own travel to Washington to meet President Hoover.

Given the urgent need for funding, the National Memorial Commission devised a plan to obtain federal support for the memorial building. At the meeting with President Hoover in December of 1929, the commissioners made a bold request: they asked Hoover to make available two sources of federal funds long owed to African Americans. First, there were the unpaid salaries and bounties due to the African American soldiers and sailors who fought in the Civil War, but who could not be located or identified.[16]

The second claim concerned the Freedman's Bank, which was chartered by Congress at the end of the Civil War and marketed to former slaves and African American Civil War veterans as a secure place to deposit their meager savings. While the bank was federally chartered, its deposits were not federally insured. Consequently, when the bank failed in 1874, many depositors received only partial reimbursement of the amounts they had placed in their savings accounts; more than $1.2 million in deposits remained unpaid.

The claims to these bank funds were well documented, and there had been numerous requests over the years for the federal government to either pay the individual claimants or their heirs, or to make this money available for an educational or charitable project that would benefit the African American community. In the decades following the bank's failure, several congressional committees passed resolutions and introduced bills to fully reimburse Freedman's Bank depositors. Presidents Grover Cleveland and William Howard Taft also supported restitution; but ultimately, Congress failed to enact and fund such a measure.[17]

The moral claim to using these funds for the memorial building was especially compelling, given the project was inspired by the desire to honor African American veterans. One could hardly imagine a better use for funds earned by the sweat and blood of African Americans, especially in the service of defending and preserving the Union, than to construct a museum desired by those very same veterans.

When approached by Mary McLeod Bethune, President Hoover did not take kindly to the suggestion that he should take the lead on righting these historical wrongs by making these funds available. President Hoover reportedly snapped at Ms. Bethune, "That's a matter for Congress," and refused to discuss it further. [18]

At the close of the meeting, President Hoover further insulted the commissioners by refusing to pose for a photograph with them. Addison Scurlock, an African American photographer who captured images of prominent individuals and events in Washington's African American community, had accompanied the commissioners to the White House to document the occasion. The commissioners were so incensed by President Hoover's treatment they refused even to pose for a group photo without the President after the meeting.[19]

During his administration, President Hoover made it a practice not to pose with African American visitors and delegations that called on him at the White House, no matter how notable. This, his aides would say, reflected the President's concern that pictures might be misused for advertising purposes, a most curious explanation given the countless photos he took with White citizens. The African American press contrasted Hoover's treatment of distinguished Black visitors with his photographs with the most mundane of White visitors, such as Western Union messengers and Boy Scout troops.[20] Hoover did not pose with any African Americans until the end of his term, and the African American press savaged him for posing with all manner of White "ninnies and boobies," while refusing to take photos with Black dignitaries until he became desperate to "offset the great swing of Negro voters to Roosevelt."[21]

Nevertheless, the Commission remained stalwart despite the disrespect and financial insecurity it faced. It elected officers after the White House meeting, naming Ferdinand Lee its chairman, Paul R. Williams the chairman of the Sites and Plans Committee, Webster L. Porter the chairman of the Legislation Committee, and John R. Hawkins the chairman of the Ways and Means Committee.[22] In addition to the presidential appointees, Congress had specified there would be three ex-officio members of the National Memorial Commission: the Director of Public Buildings and Public Parks of the National Capital, the Supervising Architect of the Treasury, and the Architect of the Capitol. These ex-officio members attended the White House meeting and accompanied the commissioners to a meeting with Charles Moore of the Commission on Fine Arts.

At that meeting, the Commission was urged to select a site for the national memorial building near Howard University. It was a fine location, but two miles north of the National Mall where the Smithsonian complex and the most prominent memorials could be found.[23]

Meanwhile, Howard University officials expressed an interest in having the memorial building on or near its campus,[24] and the National Capital Park and Planning Commission also recommended this site. Commission members visited the spot[25] and agreed it was "an ideal location for the memorial."[26] The Commission on Fine Arts approved, stating that the Georgia Avenue site was "a wise choice and that the opportunity afforded on that site is one of the best in the city of Washington."[27] The White federal and planning officials considered this building dedicated to African American achievement as better suited for a Black neighborhood than the monumental core of the nation's capital, a sentiment expressed by David Lynn, the Architect of the Capitol, who said, "I feel that this evidences a wise selection, as the surroundings seem to be those which will make this site better adapted to do the work for which the building is to be erected."[28]

Following the 1929 White House meeting with the Commission, President Hoover had Treasury Secretary Andrew Mellon look into the matter of the federal funds due African American soldiers and Freedman's Bank depositors. Even though there was no question about the legitimacy of the claim,[29] neither Hoover nor Congress acted to make these funds available to the Commission. In fact, the Commission could not even receive a portion of their $50,000 authorization upfront.

Intense lobbying by the Commission in 1930 led the Senate to pass an amendment that would have allowed $12,500 of the federal funds to be made available immediately, but the measure did not pass the House.[30] Another bill introduced in late 1931 sought $22,500 of the Commission's appropriation, but it was likewise unsuccessful.[31] Though federal funding was desperately needed, it was nowhere in sight.

In the interim, the Commission engaged in many private fundraising activities in Washington and around the nation,[32] but the grave economic circumstances severely impeded those efforts. For instance, the Commission organized a benefit concert by Paul Robeson in 1931, the talented singer's first ever recital in Washington. The event was wildly popular and thousands attended; but with most tickets selling for one dollar or less, the fundraiser netted only $1,000 after expenses.[33]

Racial segregation also hampered the fundraising efforts. Hundreds of Black people were turned away from a 1931 benefit concert of the Hampton Choir at the Daughters of the American Revolution Constitution Hall because the White ticket agency restricted the seating of African Americans to two sections of the auditorium. As a result, most of the tickets went unsold, leading to large swaths of empty seats while legions of African Americans were unable to enjoy the performance of the famed choir and support the Commission's work.[34] These efforts, while valiant, managed to raise only a tiny fraction of the necessary funds to complete such a monumental venture.

In addition to fiscal insolvency, significant deaths[35] severely hampered the Commission's cause, and none more so than that of Ferdinand Lee,[36] the heart and soul of the movement. Shamefully, his grave bears no headstone, so there is no memorial to honor his service or to recognize the many contributions he had made to his race and to the nation, an unfortunate commonality with the Black soldiers he had championed.

Yet, the most lethal blow to the Commission came from newly elected President Franklin Delano Roosevelt.

After being sworn into the Oval Office in March 1933, President Roosevelt swiftly moved to reorganize the federal government. He abolished dozens of commissions created by Congress and President Hoover, transferring their authorities to federal agencies. One of the many bodies on the potential chopping block had been the National Memorial Commission, whose fate was sealed on June 10, 1933, when Roosevelt issued an Executive Order abolishing the Commission and transferring its duties to the Office of National Parks, Buildings, and Reservations in the Interior Department.[37] Only Congress had the power to resurrect it, but Congress failed to act.[38] The National Memorial Commission was no more.

Though the memorial building technically remained authorized, with the commission abolished the Interior Department failed to make any tangible efforts to bring the project to fruition. Other federal support for the project remained nonexistent. Roosevelt rebuffed requests from the NMA in 1934 for a $5,500 loan to cover fundraising expenses[39] and again in 1935 to construct the memorial building as a federal public works project.[40]

However, while Congress refused to fund the Black memorial building and declined to revive the National Memorial Commission, it approved a new commission to plan and construct a memorial to President Thomas Jefferson in 1934.[41] Roosevelt laid the cornerstone in 1939, and the Jefferson Memorial was completed in 1943. Congressman Rankin of Mississippi, who had opposed building a memorial to Blacks instead of one to Jefferson, was undoubtedly pleased with this turn of events.

Like Ferdinand Lee, the remaining members of the Commission passed away in the succeeding decades with the memorial dream still unfilfilled. The federal government abandoned the Commission's work, and the African American community, like the rest of the nation, turned its attention to surviving the Great Depression, supporting the country upon its entry into World War II, and witnessing the beginning of the modern civil rights movement.

With the nation having moved on, the National Memorial Building to Negro Achievement and Contributions to America was now a forgotten vision.

CHAPTER FIVE

★

A PROPOSAL WITHOUT
A PATRON

As turbulent as the 1960s were for the country, they had the coincidental effect of reviving interest in a museum to celebrate African American history and culture. The Civil Rights Movement brought with it a great interest in addressing the needs of African Americans, not only physically and civically—such as with fair housing, equal access to jobs, and suffrage—but also socially and emotionally. Those within the movement began to promote the importance of providing African Americans with a sense of self-worth and buy-in to their national efficacy and importance. This time, however, it was a White liberal, Congressman James Scheuer, Democrat of New York, who led the charge. That raised the question of who, exactly, should be the driving force and responsible party for a national African American Museum.

In August 1965, Congressman Scheuer introduced a bill to create a "Negro History Museum Commission," appointed by President Lyndon Baines Johnson, that would study the advisability of establishing such a museum and report within six months.[1] The bill did not receive significant support from the African American community, and the House did not act on it.

In fact, many African Americans did not embrace the notion of a federal Black history museum. African American Congressman Adam Clayton Powell, Democrat from Harlem, New York City, represented many grassroots organizations when he spoke against the concept, saying, "[W]hether or not such a monument—a museum of Negro history—is constructed should depend on the Negros themselves. The impetus must come from within the Negro community, not from outside it."[2] Likewise, African

American congressmen from Boston, Detroit, and Chicago expressed concerns about establishing a national museum as these cities already housed several museums and cultural institutions dedicated to Black history and culture. They felt that a federal effort could detract or draw support away from these local endeavors.

The failure of the bill did not end interest in the issue. During one week in June 1967, as the nation reeled from back-to-back race riots in Tampa, Cincinnati, and Buffalo, six nearly identical bills were introduced to establish a Negro History Museum Commission. They met the same fate as Congressman Scheuer's 1965 bill: no hearing and no vote.

Undeterred, a group of congressmen led by Scheuer introduced a slightly modified bill in August 1967. This proposed bill also sought to establish a "Commission for the Study of Negro History and Culture," however, this commission would study how to preserve and collect African American historical and cultural materials. Then it would devise means to disseminate and integrate such materials into mainstream American media, culture, and education. It would also examine whether to establish a museum or create an institution to share and promote "Negro history and culture."[3] The bill did not receive a hearing in 1967, but it finally gained an audience in March 1968 before the House Select Subcommittee on Labor.

The House committee would meet on March 18, 1968, just three weeks after the issuance of the seminal report by the National Advisory Commission on Civil Disorders, otherwise known as the Kerner Commission, after its chair, Governor Otto Kerner of Illinois. President Lyndon Baines Johnson established the Kerner Commission to study the causes of the dozens of bloody race riots in the summer of 1967 and to recommend a cure. In its report, the Kerner Commission ominously concluded that "our nation is moving toward two societies, one Black, one White—separate and unequal," a verdict that appeared on the front page of newspapers all over the country. The Rev. Dr. Martin Luther King, Jr. called the Kerner Report "a physician's warning of approaching death [of the nation,] with a prescription for life."[4]

As the specter of the Kerner Report loomed, this hearing became a microcosm of the national debate about and within the Black community. First, there was the question of what people of African descent should be called. Roy Innis of the Congress of Racial Equality (CORE) criticized the name of the proposed commission. As a self-proclaimed "Black nationalist," Innis argued the country was moving away from the term "Negro" and admonished Congress to change the commission's name from Negro to Black or African American.

In contrast, NAACP official John Morsell maintained that Negro was a "good word" for describing Black Americans so long as it was capitalized.[5] Morsell noted it had taken twenty-five years to get the word capitalized in general usage; he did not want that effort wasted, especially as he did not believe there was an overwhelming consensus for "Black" instead of "Negro." He also noted that at the time of the NAACP's establishment in 1909, there was deliberation over using the term "Afro-American," "Colored," or "Negro" and he questioned the value of continuing the debate six decades later.[6]

Second, there was the issue of who should take part in the proposed commission. Innis asserted that in order for it to have credibility within the Black community, a committee of Black leadership, rather than the White President, should appoint the members of the commission. He also insisted that all of the commission's members should be Black so it would be "composed of the people who are most affected by this problem, Black people."[7] Once again, Morsell disagreed with Innis, preferring the commission be an integrated body.[8]

Last, opinions differed about the federal government's role with the proposed commission. Dr. Charles Wright, founder of the International Afro-American Museum[9] (IAM) in Detroit, was skeptical of creating yet another commission to address African American issues. Dr. Wright, a Black gynecologist, had launched the Detroit museum in 1965 shortly after returning from Alabama, where he had rendered medical treatment to the civil rights protestors who had been bludgeoned while trying to cross the Edmund Pettus Bridge in Selma.[10]

Wright's vision was that the IAM could eventually become a national museum, so the bills introduced in Congress presented an obstacle.[11] Wright observed the Kerner Commission report was already gathering dust; and, in his view, that report simply a rehashed a 1922 anti-riot commission report that followed the 1919 Chicago race riots. Dr. Wright urged, "[T]he story of the [N]egro cannot wait for that. We have to have actions,"[12] and suggested Congress fund grassroots efforts like his rather than create a new commission.

By contrast, Dr. Charles Wesley, a protégé of Carter G. Woodson who succeeded Woodson as the executive director of the Association for the Study of Negro Life and History, noted his organization was one of the primary engines behind this bill. Dr. Wesley did not support a separate Negro history museum, which he viewed as a form of segregation, and instead advocated for integrating Black history as "part of the whole scheme of things."[13] He stressed the importance of the commission in helping to change the image of the Negro in America "by constructing the [N]egro into a person, into an American," and contended "all we are asking in this bill is that the commission give an opportunity for the Negro to occupy an equal place in history with the other peoples who have helped to develop this nation, because America is ours."[14]

Notwithstanding these disagreements, there was widespread favorable consensus for the bill's central purpose: promoting the study of Black history and culture.

Dr. John A. Davis of the American Society of African Culture argued the commission was needed to remedy the psychological effects of slavery, segregation, and miseducation because "[t]he Negro lives in a culture where White is brilliant, White is efficient, White is right, White is powerful, White is rich, White is knowledgeable—and the Negro is nothing."[15] Melvin Goode, a television news correspondent, agreed, quoting Dr. Martin Luther King, Jr.'s "Letter from a Birmingham Jail," that "[Negroes] are forever fighting a degenerating sense of nobody-ness," and White people must understand and appreciate the comradeship, cooperation, and help of the Black man in building the nation and society.[16]

Congressman Scheuer echoed the sentiments of these witnesses, noting schoolbooks and the media failed to educate Americans on African Americans' contributions to the nation and stating, "[W]e must remedy this situation and this oversight...and this moral debt that America owes to the Negro in terms of giving him the way to enjoy a self-image that is rightfully his."[17]

Nearly all of the witnesses stated the commission should focus on promoting the research and dissemination of Black history in textbooks and the media instead of creating a museum.

One of the bill's most prominent supporters was Jackie Robinson, the baseball Hall of Famer who broke the color barrier in Major League Baseball. At the March hearing, he observed many "sins of commission" had been committed against African Americans, including exploitation, racial discrimination, and violence. But he also asserted that the "sins of omission" had been just as bad:

[O]ne of the major sins of omission has been the failure of historians and educational authorities to assign to Black Americans the credit they richly deserve for the collective and individual contributions they have made to American history and culture and to the growth of this country.[18]

Noting also that certain congressmen were attempting to block the Civil Rights Housing Bill, and that the U.S. Olympic Committee was supporting apartheid South Africa's participation in the 1968 Summer Olympics,[19] Robinson continued, "I am as frustrated and angry as everyone[;] there have been times when I felt like getting into the streets myself."[20]

Still, Robinson believed the bill presented an opportunity for Congress and the federal government to do something positive for the African-American community, such as providing jobs for young Black people. He said, "If we can get them to understand that we do care, they might go into these jobs rather than go into these communities to stir up that trouble..."[21]

Perhaps the most insightful and provocative witness to appear at the hearing was writer and social critic James Baldwin.[22] The bestselling author of *The Fire Next Time* supported creating the Commission, but he warned Congress that "my history...contains the truth about America. It is going to be hard to teach it."[23] Baldwin maintained that even though the task was difficult, it was nonetheless essential. "If we are going to build a multiracial society, which is our only hope, then one has got to accept that I have learned a lot from you and a lot of it is bitter, but you have a lot to learn from me and a lot of that will be bitter. That bitterness is our only hope. That is the only way we get past it."[24]

He explained that White and Black America were interconnected and could not be separated. "I am the flesh of your flesh and bone of your bone; I have been here as long as you have been here—longer—I paid for it as much as you have. It is my country too. Do recognize that that is the whole question. My history and culture has got to be taught. It is yours."[25]

When asked whether the commission should study contemporary heroes as well as past Black heroes, Baldwin cautioned, "Yes, but you must understand that, speaking as Black Americans, my heroes have always been from the point of view of White Americans...'bad niggers.' Cassius Clay[26] is one of my heroes but not one of yours."

The mention of contemporary Black people caused Baldwin to push the point even further. As some of his most famous works had been influenced by martyred African Americans, such as Emmett Till, Medgar Evers, and Malcolm X, Baldwin demanded the commission study "why all my heroes came to such bloody ends."[27]

Baldwin's observation was prescient. Seventeen days after the hearing, Dr. King was assassinated in Memphis, Tennessee. Jackie Robinson was named the head of a private organization in support of the Negro History Commission on that very day, in a hurried effort to provide some meaningful response to the assassination.[28] The effort was futile, as mass unrest enveloped the nation in the days and weeks following King's assassination. Despite the Kerner Report, the cycle of rioting that had plagued the summer of 1967 repeated itself yet again.

Months later, the Senate held a hearing that would pick up where the House Committee left off. Senator Hugh Scott, a Republican from Pennsylvania, introduced a bill that was nearly identical to the House bill. He, Congressman Scheuer, and the Association for the Study of Negro Life and History worked together to organize a one-day conference on Capitol Hill to publicize and build support for their legislative efforts.[29]

Senator Scott pointed out that "[t]he almost total absence of awareness of the Negro as a valuable contributor to our society—something approaching an inadvertent conspiracy—has gone on for so long that we will have to undertake a very considerable effort to make up for several hundred years of neglect."[30] He also noted, "The African cultural heritage of the United States, from coffee and chocolate to the latest teenage dance steps, has been fully assimilated into the American scene, and is taken totally for granted."[31] In Senator Scott's words, "Negligence of the Negro role in American history is both the cause and the effect of prejudice today."[32]

The media's power was a central focus of the Senate hearing. A few days prior, CBS had broadcast *Black History: Lost, Stolen, or Strayed*, a television special that featured discussion on prominent people and events in Black history, as well as on the portrayals of Black people in television and film, including *Uncle Tom's Cabin* and *The Birth of a Nation*. Senator Scott entered the program's entire script into the Senate hearing record. He also introduced several articles and columns from magazines and newspapers that explained how constant negative stereotypes of Black people and the absence of Black history in education adversely affected Black children's self-esteem and self-efficacy while it perpetrated White people's racism and prejudice.

Julius Hobson, a community leader based in Washington, D.C., testified that because he never learned about Black history as a youngster, he had suffered from low self-image as a member of the Air Force during World War II:

[I felt I] really had nothing to offer and I was ashamed of everything that I had been and everything I had done, because I had not been exposed to any Black history. I did not think Negroes could do anything but cook.[33]

He believed teaching Black history in schools could inspire Black pride, Black identity, and Black positivity in younger generations, and he hoped "less palatable" Black people like himself or Stokely Carmichael, who were part of the Black Power Movement,[34] could be involved in the commission.

Ronald Bailey—a Black student from Michigan State University who worked as a congressional aide—favored the commission as long as it reflected the will of the Black community by hiring Black historians and supporting existing Black institutions.[35] He advocated for calling the commission "Afro-American" because doing so would acknowledge the African roots. He thought Negro often evoked the period of time from slavery onward, "a period that is still a badge of shame for many [B]lack Americans."[36]

Officials from the Schomburg Center for Research in Black Culture in New York[37] and the Howard University Library hoped the commission would create a funding stream to support their efforts. Both institutions asserted that lack of funding prevented them from collecting and properly preserving documents related to Black history, and they often lost talented staff because of their inability to pay decent wages. Numerous letters, articles, and reports were also entered into the record discussing the importance of studying Black history and the rise of the "Black studies" movement.

The Senate committee requested all federal agencies provide reports of their activities in educating the public about Black history or preserving and documenting Black history and culture. Agencies such as the Library of Congress and the National Archives provided responses that were entered into the record; however, the Smithsonian Institution did not provide a report or send a representative to present testimony. If it had had any interest in the proposed commission, the Smithsonian failed to show it.[38]

In September 1968, the commission bill came up for debate and vote in the House of Representatives. Leading the opposition was Congressman Joe Waggonner, Democrat of Shreveport, Louisiana, who had been president of his community's White Citizens' Council.[39] He contended the commission would "cause more discord"[40] than harmony, reflecting the prevailing view among Southern congressmen that the study of Black history could encourage "race hate," Black power, or other so-called radical doctrines.[41] Despite the opposition, the bill passed the House by a significant majority; however, the measure died in the Senate, again dashing hope for establishing the commission.[42]

A separate campaign to promote Black history sought to gain a foothold in Congress. Days after King's assassination, Congressman Clarence

Brown announced legislation to create a national museum and repository of Black history and culture in his home district of Wilberforce, Ohio. Brown believed the riots and unrest that had followed King's death "attest[ed] to the idea that our nation needs the reconciliation between the races which can be fostered by the museum I have proposed."[43]

However, Brown's legislation did not get traction until 1976, when his bill received a House hearing and a companion bill received a Senate hearing. Brown argued Wilberforce was a suitable location for a national museum because the town was founded in the 1830s by manumitted Black people and had been a center of the abolitionist movement and a station on the Underground Railroad. Moreover, two local historically Black universities—Wilberforce University and Central State University—had pledged their support. Brown even boasted that Colonel Charles Young, the famed West Point graduate and Buffalo Soldier, had taught in the local high schools and at Wilberforce University.[44] Ironically, Brown was likely unaware of Young's refusal to participate in the National Memorial Association's efforts to create a museum six decades prior due to his disgust with the nation's failure to pass anti-lynching and anti-discrimination laws.

Senator John Glenn, the celebrated former astronaut,[45] supported his fellow Ohioan's proposal.[46] Glenn also highlighted the significance of Black historical events that took place in Wilberforce, in order to justify placing the national museum there rather than in the nation's capital or somewhere else. He argued the museum was necessary because it would inspire all Americans and "serve as a national restatement of our goal [of assuring Black] history and past and present achievements in culture are thought of and are treated as an integral, vital part of our whole society."[47]

The Ohioans had the support of their state legislature, which had created the National Museum of Afro-American History and Culture Planning Council to plan for a museum in Wilberforce and appropriated $80,000 to the council.[48] The proponents even struck a patriotic theme during the Congressional hearings, noting it would be fitting for America to honor its Black citizens and their contributions to the nation during the country's bicentennial year.

The House and Senate bills also proposed the new national museum would be a part of the National Park Service, but this proved to be controversial. Dr. Richard Curry, a National Park Service official, acknowledged that while the museum was "an idea of great genius, an idea whose time has come," his agency believed it was ill-equipped to be responsible for the museum[49] because the National Park Service was better suited for the task of preserving historical sites rather than administrating museums.

Without naming any specific entity, the Secretary of Interior requested Congress designate "a more appropriate agency" to establish the museum.[50] It was likely lost history that the Department of Interior had been given responsibility to create the National Memorial Building to Negro Achievement and Contributions to America when Franklin D. Roosevelt abolished the National Memorial Commission in 1934.

None of the bills introduced from 1968 to 1976 to create the Wilberforce museum passed, but museum supporters achieved a partial victory in 1976 when Congress directed the Secretary of the Interior to "study the feasibility/suitability of a National Museum of Afro-American History and Culture at or near Wilberforce, Ohio."[51]

The National Park Service study concluded that Wilberforce was an appropriate location for a major historic site, but not for a national museum, and that the Smithsonian Institution should run any such museum if it were ever created.[52] At the time, however, the Smithsonian had no interest in creating a separate museum dedicated to African-American history and culture. Its preferred strategy was to incorporate African-American history into its existing establishments.[53] Without the Smithsonian's support, the proposed National Afro-American Museum had no willing federal patron.

In response to the impasse, Congress created yet another commission. In 1980, the National Afro-American History and Culture Commission was established to develop "a definitive plan for the National Center for the Study [of] Afro-American History and Culture" in Wilberforce. The Commission's purpose was to examine how the center could be funded and how it should relate to federal agencies, and then report the plan to Congress within two years.[54]

As in 1929, the Commission was not allocated funds and so could not properly discharge its duties. Five years later, at Senator Glenn's urging, Congress finally appropriated $200,000 to this newest commission; but congressional support for the Wilberforce museum had by then withered.[55]

Meanwhile, the State of Ohio proceeded with its plan to create a "national" museum in Wilberforce. In 1988, the 50,000–square foot National Afro-American Museum and Cultural Center opened in Wilberforce without any official Congressional designation as a "national museum."

The next year, Congress approved the National Museum of the American Indian, specifying it be part of the Smithsonian Institution and built on the National Mall, in a structure no smaller than 400,000 square feet.[56]

Any plans for Congress to create a national museum dedicated to Black history, whether in Washington or anywhere else, remained in disarray nearly six decades after the passage of the 1929 legislation. Indeed, with each succession of underfunded and ineffective commissions in the 1970s and early 1980s, the vision articulated by Ferdinand Lee and the National Memorial Association was slowly fading, inching toward an inevitable death under the weight of legislative and bureaucratic apathy.

CHAPTER SIX

★

ENTER JOHN LEWIS—
AND THE SMITHSONIAN

As Congress dithered in the 1980s about whether to establish a National Afro-American Museum in Wilberforce, yet another plan emerged to build a national museum in Washington. This time, the Smithsonian would not be able to remain on the sidelines.

The man behind the new plan was Thomas Mack, a successful entrepreneur and the quintessential American success story. Mack started as a tour guide with Universal Studios in Los Angeles, and he worked his way up to a management position within the company. In the 1970s, Universal asked Mack to draft a proposal for providing a tour bus service around the monuments and museums of the National Mall, similar to the trolleys that drove tourists around the Hollywood studios and movie sets. Mack not only wrote the proposal, but he went to Washington to sell the Park Service on the idea. He won them over, and once the Park Service awarded the contract to Tour Mobile, Mack went to Washington to run the operation. In 1981, he bought the company from Universal. As CEO of Tour Mobile, Mack had a unique perspective on the National Mall. Daily, he saw how the monuments and museums dedicated to America's heroes and triumphs impacted visitors from all over the world. He recognized the potential significance if tourists also had greater exposure to African American history and culture.

In 1984, Mack formed an organization called the National Council for Education and Economic Development (NCEED). Mack used his Hollywood, business and political connections to build support for NCEED, and within a few years, the organization had the support of a broad range of heavy hitters, including Lena Horne (its Honorary Chairwoman), Carl Rowan Jr., Willie Brown, Dorothy Height, Vernon Jordan, Alex Haley, Dr. Alvin Poussaint, Arthur Ashe, O.J. Simpson, Bill Cosby, Quincy Jones, B.B. King, Gladys Knight and the Pips, Patti Labelle, and Stevie Wonder. NCEED also gained the support of several historically Black colleges and universities and educators from predominantly White institutions.

During this time, Congressman Mickey Leland, Democrat of Texas, pushed Congress to acknowledge and promote Black history. In 1985, Leland introduced a bill to create the "American Slavery Memorial Council" that would build a museum, modeled on the Holocaust Museum, in remembrance of America's original sin.[1] That bill failed to gain a hearing or a vote. However, Leland was an NCEED supporter, and the separate effort he coordinated with NCEED had more success.

In 1986, Leland led the effort for Congress to pass, and have President Reagan sign, a joint resolution to "encourage and support" NCEED in its efforts to raise a private endowment to establish a "commemorative structure" within the National Park System or on other federal lands dedicated to African American history and culture.[2]

This resolution was intended to lay the groundwork for NCEED to begin raising funds to build a national museum, hopefully on the National Mall, dedicated to African American history and culture. Unfortunately, the resolution was merely a suggestion that expressed the "sense of the Congress" and, while positive, it was worth little more than the paper on which it was printed.

NCEED needed a formal mandate from Congress to establish such a museum. Regrettably, the 1929 creation of the National Memorial Commission and authorization of the National Memorial Building to Negro Achievement had been forgotten, so Leland and NCEED were setting the stage for another lengthy battle to create a museum that Congress had already approved decades earlier.

But the resolution was a start, and Mack moved forward with great determination. In April 1988, NCEED sponsored a star-studded concert at the Kennedy Center featuring Patti Labelle and Lena Horne.[3] And in September, NCEED's efforts generated another tangible step forward.

John Lewis, the civil rights hero of the 1960s and now a freshman member of Congress from Georgia, introduced a bill to create a "National African American Heritage Museum and Memorial." The bill specified that even though this would be a Smithsonian museum, it would be run by a 15 member "independent" board of trustees consisting of at least 7 officers of

NCEED, and that the board would "maintain and administer the museum through [NCEED]."[4]

During this time, Mack imagined locating the museum on the National Mall, between the Smithsonian's Air and Space Museum and the Botanical Gardens Building on the Capitol grounds. However, Mack did not know that over a dozen years earlier Congress had quietly designated that spot, bounded by Third and Fourth Streets on the southern side of the National Mall,[5] and that many had envisioned it as a site for a future Smithsonian museum dedicated to the American Indian.[6] This was quite a dilemma, because Mack and the others wanted a museum to be located on the National Mall, and the conventional wisdom at the time was that this location was the last available site for a new building on the Mall.

When Mack learned of the Smithsonian's plans, he hoped the African American and Indian museums could share the site,[7] and Lewis' 1988 bill formally endorsed creating the American Indian museum along with the African American museum. However, no action was taken on Lewis' bill, so the matter would have to wait for the next session of Congress.

In 1989, Representatives Lewis and Leland introduced nearly identical bills to create a "National African American Heritage Memorial Museum." The two bills, similar to Lewis' 1988 legislation, specified that the museum would be under the umbrella of the Smithsonian, but run by an "independent" board of trustees. The bills weakened the power of NCEED, giving it only 7 of 19 seats on the board, and omitting the requirement that the board administer the museum "through NCEED."[8]

Mack did not trust the Smithsonian. He did not believe the Smithsonian, lacking the commitment to African American history in general, or to creating a national African American museum in particular, could be trusted to manage this project. Mack was not alone.

Earlier that year, the House of Representatives had held a scathing hearing on the minority hiring practices of the Smithsonian, which laid bare the dearth of minorities in leadership positions throughout the institution. Congresswoman Cardiss Collins concluded that "[g]iven the Smithsonian's homogenous power structure, it is perhaps not surprising that minority interests have been slighted in museum exhibits, displays, and other activities."[9]

John Kinard, the director of the Smithsonian's Anacostia Museum, was direct in his assessment of his own institution's leadership: they were racist and would never support sufficient resources for his Anacostia museum or the creation of a national African American museum on the mall.[10]

At a September 1989 hearing on Lewis' bill, Smithsonian Secretary Robert McCormick Adams did little to disabuse skeptics when he testified that building a wing on an existing museum to study African American history might be preferable to establishing a new standalone museum devoted to the subject.[11]

Congressman Lewis, who was now the primary museum advocate in the House following Leland's tragic death in an August 1989 plane crash, called Adams' idea "simply unacceptable and demeaning. The story of Black Americans is so rich that it must be told in a world-class setting and not in a wing attached to some building."[12]

Lewis Harland, President of the American Historical Association and the Organization of American Historians, agreed, noting that "Black people have a unique history in America of toil and trouble, of achievement, and institutional development that is not easily translatable or subsumable under a generalized American national experience; it is unique."[13]

Mack was equally critical, noting that "[a] wing is tantamount to the Smithsonian's personification of African Americans as second-class citizens, and that may be very well consistent with Smithsonian attitudes toward minorities if its history is an accurate barometer of [its] behavior and beliefs."[14]

In addition to the role and control of the Smithsonian, two other issues arose at the September 1989 hearing that would foreshadow trouble for Lewis' legislation. One was the potential impact the national museum may have on local African-American museums, a criticism that had arisen in the late 1960s. The Lewis bill responded by establishing a trust fund to support local museums. Edmund Barry Gaither, President of the African American Museums Association provided qualified support, endorsing the bill only so long as it included this proviso, arguing that the national trust was essential to ensure that the new museum would have a positive and constructive effect on local museums.[15]

The other controversial issue was the size and location of the museum building. Lewis' 1988 bill specified that the museum must comprise at least 377,000 square feet and be located on the National Mall. The 1989 bill kept the size requirement, but it stated that the museum could be located on either the National Mall or any other available federal lands in Washington.

At the September 1989 hearing, Robert E. Gresham, an official with the National Capital Planning Commission, testified that if, as anticipated, the National Museum of the American Indian was constructed, that was "widely considered by many to be the last available site on this Mall proper area for a major, independent, freestanding museum."[16] He therefore urged Congress not to specify that the African American museum must be located on the Mall, but rather to state that it be placed on a "suitably prominent site nearby or adjacent."[17]

This position caused great consternation to museum supporters, all of whom desired a Mall location. The consternation grew just after Thanksgiving, when Congress authorized the National Museum of the American Indian at the aforementioned "last available" site on the Mall, with the active encouragement of the Smithsonian.[18]

At the September 1989 hearing on Lewis' bill, Smithsonian Secretary Adams testified that he was not taking a formal position on the legislation and was appearing "primarily in a listening and learning posture."[19] But the pressure was mounting on the Smithsonian to take a stand on a national African American museum, particularly given its support for the American Indian museum. In December 1989, Secretary Adams appointed Claudine K. Brown as the director of what was called the African American Institutional Study Project, tasked to determine how to implement the Smithsonian's African American "presence" on the mall.

Brown was a very talented and respected professional, with a master of science in museum education and a law degree. She would need all of her skills and then some to manage the competing factions, historical distrust, and political traps that had bedeviled this project for decades.[20]

Brown assembled a powerful and accomplished committee of advisors to help her compile the study. The Institutional Study Committee was chaired by Mary Schmidt Campbell who, as the Commissioner of Cultural Affairs for New York City, was the highest-ranking African American public arts administrator in the country. The committee wisely included representation of local African American museums with the addition of Joy Ford Austin, the President and Executive Director of the African American Museums Association.

Secretary Adams was cognizant of the fears of the local African American museums, noting that they were not "anxious to have a giant vacuum cleaner appear on the Mall and suck them dry of financial support and material,"[21] and he wanted the Committee to confront those issues head-on and seek consensus. The Committee had an impressive array of persons with backgrounds in museums, history, arts, culture, humanities, business and law.[22]

In 1991, following several meetings and an in-depth study by expert consultants, the Smithsonian Institutional Study Committee concluded that "[t] here exists no single institution devoted to African Americans which collects, analyzes, researches and organizes exhibitions on a scale and definition comparable to those of the major museums devoted to other aspects of American life."[23] Consequently, the Committee concluded: 1) that a national museum dedicated to African American history and culture was needed, 2) that the museum should be a part of the Smithsonian and governed by the Smithsonian Board of Regents, with a mostly advisory and predominantly African American governing board, modeled after the Board of the National Museum of the American Indian, 3) that the museum should be established in the 100 year old, 177,000 square foot Arts & Industries Building on the Mall, with long term plans for a new, larger facility and 4) that there should be a National Trust to assist existing regional African American museums.

While the Committee report was generally well received by most of the museum supporters in Congress, there was concern due to the Smithsonian's demonstrated poor track record on presenting African American history and culture and in hiring and retaining African American employees.[24] But the Smithsonian's Board of Regents endorsed the Committee's findings, and, for the first time, the Regents were formally behind creating a stand-alone national African American museum.

Congressman Lewis, working with Senator Paul Simon, Democrat of Illinois, drafted a bill adopting the Committee's plan of action; however, in response to objections by some in Congress, Lewis and Simon eliminated the creation of the museum trust, in favor of tasking the Institute for Museum Services, an existing federal grant-making body, to report on how it could support local African American museums and then seek to fund such grants in the next appropriations cycle. In addition, the bill included language creating an affiliates program, so that local African American museums could have a formal relationship with the new national museum.[25] The African American Museums Association (AAMA) formally supported the compromise, but the situation was tenuous, as there was still concern within the local museum community.

It appeared that success was on the horizon. During Black History Month in 1992, museum advocates achieved an important milestone: receiving the Smithsonian's formal support for a bill introduced in Congress. Some even optimistically believed that the museum could open in the Arts and Industries Building by 1996.[26]

But not everyone was happy with this turn of events.

Tom Mack, who helped get the ball rolling in the 1980s, was a glaring omission from the Institutional Study Committee. Secretary Adams did not trust Mack, and Mack certainly did not trust Adams. Mack believed that the only way that the Smithsonian should be involved was in name only, and that the governance of the museum should be independent, similar to the structure of the National Gallery of Art and the John F. Kennedy Center for the Performing Arts.

However, these two independent entities were the result of hard bargaining by Andrew Mellon, who donated his art collection and paid for the construction of the National Gallery, and by the Kennedy family, which supported establishment of the memorial for an assassinated and beloved President. None of the other Smithsonian museums, including the newly established American Indian museum, had independent boards, and the proponents of the African American museum did not have the leverage of formidable fortune or a nation's grief to force another exception to the general rule. None of that mattered to Mack, who argued that the Smithsonian was "incapable" and should not be trusted to control this museum, because "they have a racist history that is 143 years long [and] whatever their attitude is now is simply a result of circumstances that required them to get involved."[27]

Mack also objected to the Smithsonian-endorsed plan to place the museum in the Arts and Industries Building, which was more than 100 years old and the second most aged building on the Mall. Mack argued that it added insult to injury to create a museum that would be much smaller than the planned American Indian and Holocaust Museums. In Mack's view, the Committee members had deferred too much to the Smithsonian and had chosen an expedient location rather than the best one.[28]

Others shared Mack's concerns. Prominent Black columnist Carl Rowan Jr. also criticized the Arts and Industries Building as too old and too small, arguing that "Americans deserve better. They deserve a first-class African American heritage museum on the Mall."[29]

Mack's opposition to the Committee and its recommendations became ammunition for a split within museum advocates about the path forward. Congressman Gus Savage led the charge against the Committee's findings. Savage attended the 1992 conference of the AAMA and verbally attacked the Black participants and supporters of the Institutional Study Committee, essentially calling them Uncle Toms, prompting some of those present to storm out of the session.[30]

At a House hearing on Lewis' bill, Savage cross-examined Secretary Adams as if he were a criminal defendant on trial, peppering him with questions as to why the National African American Museum was not worthy of a fine new building on a large site with landscaped grounds like the National Museum of the American Indian or the Holocaust Museum.

Congressman Savage proposed placing the museum on vacant land between 14th and 15th Streets and Independence and Madison Avenues on the south side of the Mall, near the Washington Monument.[31] Savage noted that this site was vacant, available, and right across the street from the Holocaust Museum, but a representative of the National Capital Planning Commission responded that the commission's "current thinking is that it might better remain open space."[32]

The Secretary and the Institutional Study Committee were between a rock and a hard place. As James Early, a Black Assistant Secretary of the Smithsonian would later note, the Arts and Industries Building "could have been claimed, and then in future years we could have figured out other options. But by putting forth an abstract ideological argument, which avoids the practical twists and turns, we end up with absolutely nothing."[33]

The disagreement and confusion about the best site for the museum proved nearly fatal.

While 1992 saw another milestone, as the Senate passed Senator Simon's bill to create the National African American Museum in the Arts and Industries Building, this achievement could not be reached in the other chamber. Savage maneuvered House rules to kill the legislation in his committee, and Lewis' bill could never get a vote. Amid scandal, Savage had already been defeated in the 1992 Democratic primary by this time, so he was on his way out of the Congress. Even though he was a lame duck, Savage chose to use his remaining time in power to prevent this project from moving forward.

In 1993, with Savage now gone, and despite the lack of support of Tom Mack and NCEED, Congressman Lewis was able to get his museum bill to the House floor for a vote, and it passed without objection.[34] As in the year before, the bill authorized the creation of the museum in the Arts and Industries Building until a larger, new facility could be constructed.

But just as the mood had changed in the House, it had also changed in the Senate. When Senator Simon brought his bill up for a vote in 1992, he was able to do so by voice vote.[35] By 1993, Senator Jesse Helms, Republican of North Carolina, was a steadfast opponent of Simon's bill. Pointing to Helms' past actions, including opposition to desegregation,[36] opposition to the national holiday for Rev. Dr. Martin Luther King,[37] and a racially charged 1990 Senate campaign against Black challenger Harvey Gantt,[38] some questioned Helms' motives.

Others noted that Helms had lost a high-profile fight with Democrat Carol Moseley Braun, the first African American female Senator, over what had previously been a routine re-authorization by Congress of the approval of a Congressional Seal for the United Daughters of the Confederacy, and therefore suggested his opposition to the museum was payback.[39]

For his part, Helms stated that his primary objection to the museum was its potential cost. He held up action in the Senate Rules Committee for several months by demanding answers to a lengthy list of questions he had sent to the Smithsonian about the museum and its cost. By 1994, the Smithsonian had pared back its proposal so that the museum would open in the Arts and Industries Building on a small scale. The Smithsonian vowed to shift around its resources so that the creation of the museum would not increase its annual operating expenses, and it pledged to raise any additional funds through private sources. None of that changed Helms' opposition.[40]

In addition to cost, Helms attacked the mission of the museum and the rationale behind its creation. He argued that once this museum was approved, Hispanics and every other minority group would want a museum and that Congress would not be able to say no to all of those groups. Helms rejected the findings of the Institutional Study Committee and other experts, for he contended that the museum was not really needed, since there were exhibits relating to African Americans in the Anacostia Museum, the National Museum of American History, and other Smithsonian museums. Helms also raised concerns about the content of this potential museum, such as whether it would contain exhibits that would "demonize America."[41]

In 1994, the Senate Rules Committee finally approved the museum bill by a vote of 10-0, with the support of 6 Democrats and 4 Republicans. Helms skipped the vote, but sent a proxy to the committee meeting stating that he would have voted against it had he been present. Afterwards, Helms put a hold on the bill, meaning the Senate would have to find a time in its schedule to debate the bill and obtain a supermajority to invoke cloture.[42] Simon was never able to muster sufficient votes to get his bill passed.

The tag team obstruction of Savage and Helms had succeeded in stymieing the effort.

The combination of Helms' steadfast opposition and the fiscal conservatism of the new House Republican majority that came to power in the 1994 elections gave museum proponents little hope that they would be able to navigate a bill through Congress when the new session began in 1995.

Adams left the Smithsonian, and the new Secretary, Michael Heyman, summed up the prevailing attitude when he said "I wouldn't have the courage to go to the legislature at least as presently constituted to ask for a new museum on the Mall," explaining that Senator Helms "puts a hold on it all the time. As we have all found out a single Senator has an enormous amount of authority to stop something."[43]

The Smithsonian further scaled back its efforts and attached the project to create the National African American Museum to the Anacostia Museum. In the eyes of many, making the national museum project an appendage of the local museum was yet another slap in the face. Dr. Thomas Battle, the director of the Moorland-Spingarn Research Center at Howard University and one of the members of the Institutional Study Committee, noted that the Anacostia Museum was a "stepchild of the Smithsonian," and he complained that the national museum project would not get sufficient visibility, funding or support in that structure.[44]

Ta-Nehisi Coates, now a bestselling author, but then relatively unknown and writing for a Washington weekly called *The City Paper*, observed that the Smithsonian had "seemingly abandoned" the museum project and that the "museum legislation has been on a congressional back burner ever since [1994]."[45] Another commentator noted, "With no help from Congress in sight, it seems that if a national Black museum is to be built in Washington, Blacks will have to do it themselves."[46]

By that time, Tom Mack and NCEED had exhausted their efforts, giving way to the next foolhardy souls to take up this seemingly lost cause.

CHAPTER SEVEN

★

AN OFFICE IN THE BASEMENT

I n 1996, with no idea the label 'foolhardy soul' would soon belong to me, my path turned toward this museum in an unexpected place: at the home of a dearly departed brother named Lewis Fraction, Sr.

A bear of a man with the confidence and boisterous nature to match, Brother Fraction's beautiful smile reached out to everyone. He always had a funny story to share, which tended to make him the life of the party.

I met him at church, as part of a 'rites of passage' program for young people, intended to aid the transition into manhood and womanhood by teaching life skills and helping the young men and women to find themselves. I served as one of the mentors for the boys and, in addition to getting to know Brother Fraction, I enjoyed the program because it allowed me to guide and support positive life choices and teach the young people how blessed they were.

Working with these young people was a welcome diversion from the depressing circumstances I encountered most days as a public defender in Washington, D.C. I found great meaning in the activities we organized. A trip behind the locked gates of the Oak Hill Youth Center, for example, though presented like a 'scared straight' session, was intended to help our youngsters understand why their parents and community members were so adamant that they go to school, stay out of trouble, and avoid drugs, alcohol, and other bad choices.

Throughout my career, I had dealt with teens and adults on the other side of those choices, and my involvement with this church activity was an early step toward the cultural empowerment the museum was created to cultivate. While I had always been troubled by the devastating circumstances of those I represented as a public defender, almost all of whom were Black or Hispanic, I started to see the big picture differently the day my wife and I visited Brother Fraction's home after his death.

Initially, Amina and I paid our respects simply because of Brother Fraction's many kindnesses. As newlyweds, having married just the year before, we looked up to Brother Fraction and his wife, Marjorie, whose decades-long marriage was a model to us of devotion and respect. As we sat with Mrs. Fraction and a number of church elders, many of whom came of age in the civil rights era, Amina and I were privileged to be welcomed into a rich conversation about cultural changes and formative experiences. We heard about courtship rituals and dance steps, about the way music evolved with the help of musicians like Sam Cooke, James Brown, and Aretha Franklin. We heard stories about what it was like when college and professional sports leagues were completely segregated, and how much things changed socially and culturally as those barriers were torn down.

At the core of these shared tales, however, amid fond memories of dedicated educators and a warm family atmosphere in their schools, the theme of 'separate but equal' stood out strongly as well. Their words, though quiet and eloquent, revealed both anger and shame at attending schools in dilapidated buildings, lacking basic educational necessities like science labs and working school buses, while White students were transported daily to brand new buildings across town.

One older gentleman recounted his surprise upon seeing a complete piece of chalk for the first time as an adult. In the segregated schools, he and his teachers used only the nubs of chalk discarded by the White schools. Black sports teams lacked basic equipment, while White teams had use of the best available. The examples went on and on. That night, I got a concrete sense, as expressed by this amazing chorus of voices, of the psychological impact of being treated as less than worthy by one's own government and so many of one's peers.

The message wasn't new to me, of course. I'd had my own difficulties along the way, growing up in Indiana amid prejudice and judgment. The son of a single mother, born when she was just seventeen, I often felt like I was less than other people, in part because we were lower middle class—and also because we were Black.

As I learned more about Black history, however, and I saw the obstacles that Black people had overcome, along with the contributions they made to our country, to science, and to other intellectual and artistic endeavors,

I began to feel better about myself. It redefined my view of America and my place within it.

That drive to learn about Black history grew even stronger in law school, where as a first-year law student at Harvard, I became chairperson of the Black history committee of the Black Law Student Association. That vantage point allowed me to remain steeped in the traditions and essential contributions of Black people, making new, meaningful discoveries along the way.

After law school, when so many of the people I represented, mostly young men in their late teens and early twenties, just seemed to have given up on themselves and their futures, the importance of that history and knowledge really hit home. When I asked youthful offenders what they wanted to be doing in five years, many of my clients told me they did not even know if they would be alive by then.

Worst of all, they did not sound sad to offer that answer. It seemed to them like a normal sentiment. It just reflected their world, and seeing that crushed me. A sixteen-year-old simply should not believe that he probably will not make it to twenty-one.

When a teenage client of mine was on the verge of dropping out, sometimes I would ask if he knew that others had marched and protested, been beaten and brought lawsuits, so that he and his contemporaries could have access to a quality education. I told these young people that they should not take those efforts, that history, for granted. The indifferent response I often received would cut me to the bone.

Later, however, when my clients were locked up, pending trial or after sentencing, they would often start reading, in part because there was little else to do, but also as an effort to better themselves. So many of them would tell me what they read, how books opened their eyes, and this led them to regret the things they had not thought about sooner, the opportunities they allowed to slip away. Even then, I had a sense that, if there was more of a connection with their history, some way for Black youths to see the sacrifices made for them and to learn how far others had come despite great obstacles, they would be more motivated to succeed and less apt to go astray.

Still, even as someone who had made the 'right choices,' I knew what it meant to be treated differently as a Black man. In 1992, while returning home from my grandfather's funeral in Chicago, three family members and I were detained by Maryland State Police so they could carry out a search by a drug-sniffing dog. That experience led to my involvement as plaintiff in a lawsuit about racial profiling—a case that went on for fifteen years.

Motivated by the 1992 search, I became active on the issue of "Driving While Black." The settlement of our lawsuit required Maryland State Police to start documenting their search practices, including the race of those searched and information on what, if anything, they had found. The resulting data showed an incredible disparity. While the number of Black people found with drugs was initially reported by the police as four times as high as the number of White people found with drugs, we were able to show that four times more Blacks were being searched in the first place. In other words, for every one hundred Blacks and one hundred Whites who were searched, the data showed that drugs were found in the same proportion. This gave credence to our argument that, even if a war on drugs was necessary, it was also necessary to treat people of all races equally.

So, by the night of this mournful gathering in honor of Brother Fraction, I was weary of feeling like I was always on defense, like I had to continually push back against obstacles, both for myself and my clients. I longed to take an offensive position, to do something proactive and productive.

And there I was that night, listening to a group of wise, experienced people who had been longing for the same proactive change as me, indeed since before my birth. Eventually, the evening's discussion revealed that, at that point in our country, things were both different and not really so different at all. People talked about the choices they made—whether or not to join certain organizations, to actively participate in the civil rights protests, to speak up despite family pressure—as well as how those decisions impacted their lives and career choices. Though I had read about so many of these topics, listening to these real life oral histories really set my mind on fire. Driving home that night, I wondered aloud to Amina, asking why there was no national museum to capture the full, unique experience of the Black American. In that question, I found purpose.

At that time, in 1996, I could not simply turn to Google for answers the way we do today. Nonetheless, I began to poke around a bit, using our home computer and a frustratingly slow dial-up internet connection. I wanted to understand whether or not there was an effort underway to create a museum, as well as to seek opportunities to lend a hand or at least donate money.

I learned that a bill to create a national African-American history museum had been introduced in 1995, and that there had been no action on it. In digging deeper, I took advantage of my widespread network of friends from law school. One of them, Cassandra Butts, worked for Congressman Dick Gephardt, Democrat of Missouri and then the minority leader of the House, and she told me that though efforts had been made over the past years, the museum bill had yet to pass, and it looked as though it had little chance of doing so in the near future. Stephanie Robinson, another friend, worked for Senator Ted Kennedy, and she gave a similar assessment. I was told that Congressman Lewis was still introducing such bills, simply for the sake of introducing them, but that no one expected them to gain traction or have a real chance of passage. When I met with Mr. Lewis and his staff, they made it clear that they were determined to keep the faith, though they acknowledged that passage of a bill was unlikely, given the political winds in Congress.

To me, that was unacceptable. I decided to gather a group of friends, people I had long identified as 'doers,' the type to roll up their sleeves and get to work. I invited them to my home for a breakfast meeting, with the purpose of brainstorming this issue. After a productive session, we agreed to meet again a couple of months later. In this way, we started meeting regularly and, within a year or two, made the decision to incorporate a nonprofit organization.

We named our new entity the National African American Museum and Cultural Complex (NAAMCC), and I took the helm as president. With a formal body, we reasoned that we could raise money, seek grant funding, and generally try to push a museum plan forward. My cousin Craig Wilkins, a very talented architect and designer, lent his expertise and advice to our group and even created a cool logo for use on our letterhead and marketing materials (figure 1).

THE NAAMCC, INC. BOARD OF DIRECTORS
Robert L. Wilkins, President
Stephanie Robinson, Vice President
Patrice Alexander Ficklin, Secretary
Jesse Fenner, Treasurer
Peter Clare
Mary Jane DeFrank
Peggy Delinois
Julie Ferguson Queen
Reverend Osagyefo Uhuru Sekou
Ronald S. Sullivan, Jr.
Dr. Cornel West

In order to craft the strongest possible plan, I dug even further into research. I spent hour after hour at the Library of Congress, where I pored through legislative history, volume by volume, to locate every bill connected in any way to what would have been called a museum for African-American, or Negro, or Colored history. I searched the records of literally every two-year Congress. I studied bills, hearings, and committee reports, as well as any newspaper articles related to those efforts. I wanted to see what had been tried, who was for it, who was against it, and what could be learned from those prior efforts.

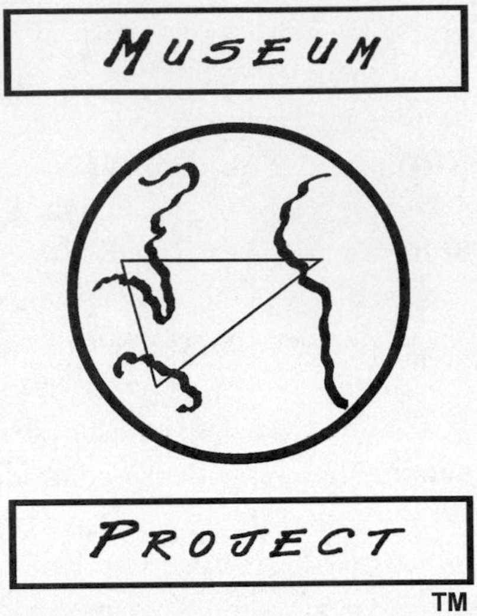

I also studied other museums. I purchased a book about efforts to create the United States Holocaust Memorial Museum and read it from cover to cover. I looked at how its founders accomplished what they did, and how they overcame their obstacles. I followed the same process to study the National Museum of the American Indian, as well as the Air and Space Museum, the National Gallery of Art, the American History Museum, and all of the various Smithsonian museums. I tried to understand who initiated them and what Congress did to create them.

I also worked to gather as many allies as I could. As a result of my research, I learned of Thomas Mack, the owner of Tourmobile, who led efforts toward the creation of an African-American history museum from the mid-1980s through the early 1990s. I contacted him, and though he was supportive, he made it clear that he was worn out and finished working on the cause.

I tracked down Claudine Brown, who led the Smithsonian's efforts in the early 1990s, and while she was sympathetic and helpful—even sending me copies of her reports and background materials—she, too, was spent after devoting years to the project. Brown's replacement as manager of the museum project for the Smithsonian, Steve Newsome, rebuffed my phone calls, so one day I just showed up at his office. In a polite—but brief—conversation, Newsome declined to join forces with my group, but we agreed to keep in contact, and my wife and I attended a fantastic gala he sponsored at the Smithsonian castle to benefit the Smithsonian's work.

I even contacted Ta-Nehisi Coates, who, at that point, was not yet a bestselling author and MacArthur "genius" grant recipient, but rather a

Figure 1: Logo

relatively unknown writer for a local weekly called the *Washington City Paper*. Coates had written a lengthy cover story in February 1998 examining "how the effort to build an African-American museum on the Mall ended up in a black hole,"[1] which described the failed efforts of the 1980s and 1990s. Though he was quite supportive of our mission and a great resource, he also offered a bleak assessment of the environment in Congress.

Hearing all of this, my group and I questioned the wisdom of putting "all of our eggs in one basket" by focusing solely on the tried (and not so true) plan of working with the Smithsonian to persuade Congress to enact a law establishing this museum on the National Mall. We got the distinct impression from Smithsonian officials that, due to past failed efforts, resistance in Congress, and the many capital needs for existing museums, they did not consider a new national African-American museum a priority.

We also knew that some civic groups and the powerful National Capital Planning Commission were actively opposed to the construction of any more museums on the Mall. Indeed, the NCPC was in the midst of drafting a master plan, which proposed establishing a strict no-build zone, called "The Reserve," on the Mall. Suffice to say, when I appeared at a public hearing on this master plan to argue that a national African American museum merited a space on the Mall, I was not warmly received.

In sum, Congress was inhospitable, the Smithsonian was noncommittal, and the Mall seemed like a long shot. But the need for this museum remained, and we remained determined to find a path forward.

So we came up with a Plan B, a plan that would not necessarily require us to get a bill through Congress, enlist the collaboration of the Smithsonian, or gain approval to build on the National Mall. We began to explore the feasibility of developing a national museum outside of the Smithsonian, and we set out to find a location for it on a prominent site, either city-owned or in private hands. We thought the museum could be created as part of a larger development, in partnership with the city, a private developer, or both. This approach was not completely without precedent, in that the United States Holocaust Memorial Museum in Washington is not operated by the Smithsonian (though a federal entity), and the African American museum in Wilberforce was established by the State of Ohio rather than the federal government.

To formulate this plan, I met with developers, city planning officials, city urban development officials, as well as various people involved in the arts, culture, and cultural tourism. Through those meetings, we identified an area in the city called Poplar Point, a forty-acre site on the banks of the Anacostia River, across from the Navy Yard and right next to a Metro subway station and a parking garage. Despite not being located on the National Mall, the Poplar Point site offered beautiful views of the Capitol dome and the city skyline. In addition, one could not deny the powerful symbolism of building this museum on the waterfront, perhaps with a slave ship replica docked right in front, within sight of the former markets, in this city and in Alexandria, Virginia, where slaves had once been bought and sold.

Though the land was federally owned and federally controlled, years of discussions had taken place between the federal government and city officials about transferring jurisdiction of Poplar Point to allow for the development the property. The city planning office had even drawn up an extensive development plan that featured a large cultural attraction on the site. But to this point, none of those plans had achieved lift-off.

Our organization hired Marshall Purnell of Devrouax & Purnell, then one of the country's largest and most prominent African American architectural firms, to draw some conceptual sketches of the museum at that site. Purnell and his designer, Anthony Brown, envisioned a soaring, iconic structure that would evoke the tragic, yet triumphant, journey of the African American community (figure 2).

National African American Museum & Cultural Complex
Waterfront Concept Sketch
Devrouax & Purnell, Architects-Planners, PC

Figure 2: Devrouax & Purnell's concept drawing

Using all of this research, we had the broad outlines of a proposal, but we needed more detailed estimates about the feasibility and cost of building a museum at Poplar Point, what public and private funding mechanisms were available, and a host of other issues. To that end, our organization applied to the city's economic development office for a grant to support our efforts. Much to our delight, our proposal was accepted, and we were awarded $150,000 to perform feasibility studies and develop a plan to make the museum a community and economic development project.

As our museum efforts continued, I was splitting my time between the non-profit work and my position as special litigation chief at the Public Defender Service, which proved especially difficult in 1997 and 1998, when the city underwent financial reconstruction and Congress created a sentencing commission to rewrite the city's sentencing and parole laws. Soon, I was knee-deep in that work, on a commission chaired by then Deputy Attorney General Eric Holder.

One thing I had learned from my research of successfully established museums, however, was that there had always been some person at some organization outside of the government working on the effort as his or her sole mission. As a result, I started to feel like our goal was not going to be realized unless someone took up that outside role. I could not find anyone else willing to do it, or who had the means to do so, and I came to realize I was going to have to be that person.

In mid-1999, after speaking to my wife, we decided that I would seek approval from my office to go to a sixty percent schedule at the Public Defender Service. This would allow me to work three days a week at my paid job and devote as much as possible of the other four days of the week to work on the museum. My request was approved, and I worked that way for a year. Still, it felt as though we just were not going to gain any traction unless I devoted myself to the museum project full time.

In August of 2000, I quit my job at the Public Defender Service to give the museum my complete focus. Most people thought I was crazy, even members of my own family. Again, though, my wife was completely supportive. She wanted to see the museum built just as much as I did. And even though she was seven months pregnant with our second child, making this quite an inopportune time to walk away from my job to run a nonprofit with no funds to pay a salary, we agreed to go for it. We had always lived below our means, and we had some savings, so we thought we could make it for a year on one salary if we scrimped even more. If we had made no progress on funding after a year, I would scale back the museum efforts and go back to gainful employment.

So I began working from my basement office with a donated computer obtained by my friend William Jordan. It was a shoestring operation at best—though probably an insult to shoestrings to label it as such. And in that year, I became very familiar with beans and cornbread.

Pressing forward was tough, and the sacrifices were not just mine. Without my job, our eldest son, Bakari, could no longer stay at his federal daycare center. Though we found a wonderful woman in the neighborhood who did home daycare, I still teared up on my first day taking him to her home, knowing we had removed him from a beautiful government daycare center just two blocks from the White House. Parents applied months, and even years, in advance for spots in those daycare centers, and we had just given away our coveted spot. While I felt certain I was not putting him in a bad situation, I did feel like I was putting my son in a lesser situation, and I wondered if I was chasing this dream at his expense.

That day, the magnitude of what I was doing hit me for the first time as I put the key in the ignition to drive back home and get to work. In that very moment, the understanding that failure was not an option crystallized in my mind. I realized that, with all of these sacrifices and changes, I had to make this museum happen.

Of course, within that year, I fully expected to receive some financial support, as we had been awarded the $150,000 grant from the economic development office to help us move forward. Those funds would have been extremely helpful, but, unfortunately, the city never paid us a dime. Though we received an official letter announcing the award, the money was never released, despite inquiries from our lawyers and numerous meetings and phone calls with city officials. Instead of money, the city gave us bountiful excuses and red tape, and we lost this battle with bureaucracy.

Soon, my family began to really feel the pain of going from two salaries to one. As I drove my mother to the airport to catch her flight home to Indiana after a visit, the engine of the family SUV suddenly began to smoke and sputter. I limped off the Baltimore-Washington Parkway to a gas station, where I used a pay phone to summon a cab to take my mom the rest of the way to the airport.

"Everything will be fine," I assured her, as she got into the taxi. She already thought I needed my head examined for quitting my job to work on this project, so this turn of events did not help my cause. As much as I tried to put on a brave face, I imagine that the tone of my voice betrayed my doubts. The look on her face certainly betrayed hers.

I got a tow truck to take me to a service station, where I received the unwelcome news that the SUV needed a new engine, at a cost somewhere between $7,000 and $10,000 with parts and labor. In one fell swoop, our nest egg was gone. This was especially traumatic, because my wife and I had already begun to realize that the cost of two kids in daycare, and all of the related family and household expenses, was making things more challenging than we anticipated. Money was tight.

Indeed, it was so tight that I could not afford a plane ticket to attend the funeral of the judge for whom I clerked, the Honorable Earl B. Gilliam, Sr. Judge Gilliam was a trailblazer, the first African American to become a state court judge, and then a federal court judge, in San Diego. He was also a gregarious and kind man, and he had given me my first legal job and launched my career. Yet I could not afford to get to California to properly pay my respects.

My idyllic vision of following passion over the practical had become a nightmare. I felt like a failure.

But we soldiered on, and God intervened to provide financial and spiritual encouragement. I was able to pick up some part-time legal work with the Public Defender Service, and with my friend Devarieste Curry, to make ends meet. And many more people, like Cornel West, agreed to lend their support to the project.

I encountered several supporters and compatriots in the strangest ways. Late one sleepless night, as I watched a jazz program on Black Entertainment Television, the musician, a White man named Mark Mitchell, spoke of his interest in Black history and of the sizable collection of documents and artifacts he had amassed in his home outside of Washington. Intrigued, I tracked down his phone number, called him the very next day, and we agreed to meet.

When I went to his home, I was astounded by his unbelievable collection. He had framed documents all over his walls, as well as countless boxes, binders, and folders full of more letters, newspapers, books, and other materials. He showed me item after incredible item, including the original of Alex Haley's publishing contract for *Roots*, a letter handwritten by Frederick Douglass about the death of Sojourner Truth, and a first edition of a work by Phyllis Wheatley, considered the first book of poetry published by an African American. It was amazing.

Mitchell's collection was obviously unique, but I came to learn that countless people all over the country had significant documents and artifacts to contribute. People were literally waiting for this museum to happen.

This knowledge gave me—and my organization—more encouragement to push forward. We held a fundraiser across the street from the Capitol building, and we displayed the beautiful conceptual sketches of the museum at Poplar Point. Attendees were overwhelmed when they saw the magnificent artifacts that Mitchell brought and displayed at the event. We wanted people to see the promise and the possibilities.

But not everyone was impressed. When asked by the *Washington Post* about our efforts, Steven Newsome of the Smithsonian said, "I think they've got a long way to go before they even figure out what they're talking about . . . What I'm trying to say is, it's hard work. When people think about these sorts of things, they have to realize these are long-term commitments and require lots of planning and lots of operational capital."[2]

Our organization still didn't have much money, and we obviously hadn't won over our many skeptics, but we had a vision, and we were committed to putting in the hard work to make this museum a reality. And though I had been knocked down, I had gotten back up, and I was still standing.

CHAPTER EIGHT

★

THE IMPROBABLE,
UNSTOPPABLE COALITION

The National Mall was a long way from the pig farm near Parker, Kansas, where Sam Brownback grew up. An avid runner, Brownback loved jogging along the Mall and admiring the beautiful monuments and museums. Aside from the exercise, these regular jogs helped the devout Senator recharge his spiritual batteries; he could pray and meditate about what it all meant and how best to serve the country as he took in the picturesque scenery.

In the spring of 2000, Brownback was deeply involved in the fight against the scourge of contemporary human trafficking, and he sponsored the groundbreaking Trafficking Victims Protection Act in the Senate, which passed Congress and was signed into law by the President later that year. As he ran past the various museums on the nation's front yard, noticing the U.S. Holocaust Memorial Museum and pondering its admonition that we should "never forget," he began to wonder why there was no museum to tell the story of the curse of American slavery, why there was nothing to ensure that our nation would never forget that horrific injustice. With that realization, he felt as if God was speaking to him, and he made a commitment to work toward the creation of such an institution.

First elected to the House in 1994, and to the Senate in 1996, Brownback missed the extensive Congressional debates over a national African American museum that took place in the 1980s and early 1990s. He soon learned that John Lewis had led those efforts in the House, and he contacted Lewis to ask if they could meet.

The meeting ran much longer than scheduled. Lewis and Brownback discussed their respective visions for a museum. While Brownback was initially focused on slavery, through their conversation, he came to support Lewis's plan of creating a national museum that told not only the story of slavery, but of the entire African American experience, including the many contributions of African Americans to our society and culture.

Lewis's office is itself practically a museum, the walls and shelves chock full of iconic photographs, memorabilia, plaques, awards, and books relating to his heroic work during the Civil Rights movement. As these two men got to know each other, Lewis pulled down a copy of *Without Sanctuary* from one of the overflowing shelves. Lewis had written the foreword for the book, which tells the story of lynching photography in America. Together, they flipped through the pages, pausing at a postcard that had been made of a lynching, in which a young White boy stood smiling for the camera while a festive White crowd and a tortured and disfigured Black man appeared in the background.

The symbolism was striking; here was a souvenir one would send or keep from a "vacation," showing the racist indoctrination of a White child and an unabashed, public, illegal execution. From that moment forward, Lewis had an ally in the Senate. But Brownback was not just any ally; he was a Republican with the political capital and the will to bring this project to fruition.

Adding to the coalition, Lewis sought the assistance of Congressman J.C. Watts, Republican of Oklahoma, with whom he had just worked successfully to pass legislation supporting the study of minority health issues by the National Institutes of Health. Like Brownback, Watts was first elected to the House in 1994. He had remained in that chamber and already become the fourth-ranking member of his party in the House as Republican Conference Chair, placing him in regular contact with the Speaker of the House and the President. Watts was eager to help; indeed Mark Mitchell, the musician and museum advocate I had met after seeing his performance on BET television, had already met with Watts to encourage him to get involved.

Lewis then recruited his fellow Georgian, Max Cleland, a first-term Senator who was himself a hero, having lost both of his legs and part of his right arm to an exploding grenade while serving in Vietnam. Cleland and Watts, like Brownback, were new to the fight for a national African American museum, but they gamely agreed to help lead the effort. Lewis, Brownback, Watts, and Cleland became our four musketeers, two from each party, and two each in the House and Senate. They became the core of the coalition to move the project forward.

Finally, we received reports that President George W. Bush, who had just taken office following a close election that was battled all the way to the Supreme Court, wanted to back the museum and that his staff would monitor our progress and push for support. So by the beginning of 2001, Lewis had amassed a formidable political coalition.

I had stayed in contact with Lewis's office, and learning of these developments convinced me and my organization to turn our focus back toward establishing this museum through Congress, particularly since our efforts on Plan B were stagnant, thanks to the non-funding of our grant by the city. I was thrilled with the progress. Forming this new coalition was truly an astounding turn of events, a real game changer. Hearing all of this, one would reasonably believe that the path to the passage of museum legislation would now be easy and straightforward.

Not so fast.

As the Four Musketeers spoke to their colleagues on the House and Senate floor, working to build support for the museum, four African American women led the corresponding efforts behind the scenes. Tammy Boyd, La Rochelle Young, Kerri Watson, and Donnice Turner were the staffers assigned to this project for Lewis, Brownback, Watts, and Cleland, respectively. They performed the vitally important, but publicly unnoticed, work of talking with the staffs of the key congressional committees, the Smithsonian, interest groups, and constituents to build support for the museum, as well as to beat back any opposition and craft detailed legislative language to achieve the objective and garner the votes to pass it.

This was no mean feat. Particularly so, because members of the Smithsonian staff made clear to them that the Institution was not in favor of the plan. They trotted out the familiar reasons: the Arts and Industries Building would not work or would be too expensive; there was no other space on the Mall for a new museum; the museum would not have a collection; Congress would not fully fund it and private donors would not make up the difference. Some Smithsonian staff members even contended that the best path forward was to build up the Anacostia Museum, which the Smithsonian Institutional Study Committee had determined was not a viable or appropriate alternative when it reviewed the issue a decade earlier. The Smithsonian staff warned that Lewis and his colleagues risked another embarrassing failure if they proceeded.

As the four congressional staff members spoke to their colleagues on the committees with jurisdiction to authorize and pay for the creation of the museum, they were met with these same points of resistance. It became apparent that the Smithsonian staff was undermining their efforts. As Lewis, Brownback, Watts, and Cleland, learned of these developments, they determined that they would have to address this problem at the member level.

The Four Musketeers summoned Lawrence Small, Secretary of the Smithsonian, and Sheila Burke, then an undersecretary and Small's right hand, to a meeting in Watts' Capitol office. Cleland was unable to attend, but Lewis and Brownback were present with Watts, together with the four staffers who had spent the preceding weeks navigating the gauntlet of opposition and doubt.

Small made his position quite clear: He was opposed to legislation that would create this new museum within the Smithsonian. The Smithsonian had too many other pressing capital needs and priorities and the bill was doomed to fail. He urged the legislators either to abandon their mission or to change course by creating the museum outside of the Smithsonian, like the Holocaust museum. In Small's view, the Smithsonian had enough problems, and it did not need what he viewed as another.

Lewis, Watts, and Brownback pushed back, noting their hard work to put together a bicameral, bipartisan coalition in support of the museum, and all of the work done over the years to answer the questions and doubts raised.

Brownback was incredulous at the Secretary's position. "Do you mean to tell me that, if we introduce this legislation, you will testify publicly to the Congress that you oppose it?" he demanded.

Small deftly responded, "I would hate to have be put in that position, Senator."

Brownback had had enough, and he walked out of the room.

Those four key staffers, Boyd, Young, Watson, and Turner, called me a few minutes after the meeting ended. I felt their anger, hurt, and frustration through the speakerphone. I, too, was devastated, though not surprised, by the outcome of the meeting. It was a punch in the gut.

But Lewis, Brownback, Watts, and Cleland had not gotten where they were in life by backing down from opposition. Besides, they knew that they had a broad base of support in Congress, plus the backing of President Bush. Indeed, Vice President Cheney had summoned them to a meeting at his office in the Capitol building to encourage and offer support for the creation of this museum.

Undaunted, they directed their staffs to continue the efforts. Mark Mitchell and several others had created a non-profit called the Friends of the

National Museum of African American History and Culture, and the Friends Group worked alongside my organization to get prominent citizens and organizations like the NAACP, the Urban League, predominantly Black fraternities and sororities, and numerous other entities to send letters to members of the House and Senate, encouraging them to support the museum.

Lewis and Brownback met with the grassroots supporters in the Longworth House Office Building to gird us for battle. Lewis recounted the commitment of the Civil Rights Movement of the 1960s, and Brownback spoke of the warrior spirit of the radical abolitionist John Brown, who had lived in the area where his mother grew up and his family still had property, a man who inspired him and his friends to play "John Brown" as kids.

To demonstrate the urgent need for Congress to finally approve and fund this institution, I shared my research showing the history of efforts to create this museum going back to 1916. The history surprised everyone involved. Up to that point, they'd all believed the efforts to create a national museum had begun no earlier than the 1960s. Staff used this history to draft talking points and "Dear Colleague" letters, encouraging members and their staff to support this museum. Enough was enough. Summing up the situation, I later penned an op-ed for the *Washington Post* entitled, "How Much Longer Must We Wait?"[1]

In the meantime, the coalition finalized the language of the companion bills to be introduced in the House and the Senate. Despite my own reservations, the consensus developed that the best way to proceed was for this museum to be operated by the Smithsonian and established in the Arts and Industries building. My organization decided to embrace that idea in order to get everyone on board because, in Washington, it is often the case that even if people have the same general goal, nothing can move forward if they disagree on the means to achieve that goal.

The House and Senate bills provided that a semi-autonomous council, consisting of twenty-five voting members and seven non-voting members, would govern the museum. I was quite proud that the principals named my non-profit as one of the organizations to advise Congress on the appointment of the council members. Most remarkable of all, I felt like I saw the best of our political system, the way it was intended to work, as we attempted to get this bill off the ground.

By May 3, 2001, the bills were ready to be introduced. The co-sponsors would include not just the original four compatriots but most of the Democratic and Republican leadership of the House, as well as Trent Lott and Harry Reid, the Majority and Minority Leaders of the Senate.[2]

Among the leafy trees and blooming flowers on the Senate side of the Capitol grounds, Lewis and company convened a press conference to announce their museum legislation and to show the deep bipartisan support for the bill. Mr. Lewis opened up by thanking Watts, Brownback, and Cleland for their leadership, and he noted that, almost exactly forty years prior to that day, he had come to Washington, D.C., for the first time, with dozens of other college students, to participate in the Freedom Rides. Then, interracial groups of young people had boarded buses headed South, testing the decision of the Supreme Court of the United States as to whether there really was freedom from racial discrimination in public transportation and public accommodations.

Forty years later, Lewis proclaimed that he and his colleagues had gathered in a similar spirit, "in a bipartisan fashion, with one mind and in one accord," to introduce the legislation to create this museum. Lewis pointed out that, even though African Americans have made vital contributions to the country, those milestones often go virtually unrecognized, and that, "until we have a complete understanding of the African American story, we cannot completely understand ourselves as a nation."[3]

Brownback added that, "one of the most important chapters in our nation's story of human freedom and dignity is the history and legacy of the African Americans and their march toward freedom, legal equality, and full participation in American society. Yet in our nation's front yard, the National Mall, there is no museum set aside to honor this legacy." He declared that, while there were over two-hundred African American museums around the country telling portions of the story, it needed to be showcased at the national level and on the Mall.

Cleland echoed this theme, observing that when he was growing up in 1950's Georgia, an African American who came to a White person's home was expected to come around to the rear and enter through the back door. He said, "Thank God we've come a long way from that," and he added, "I think that's part of what we're saying here today, that no longer does any American have to come through the back door to be a full participant in American history and in American society and citizenship."

Watts added his pleasure to be part of the effort, "to make this dream a reality," because, "African Americans have played an integral role in building this country and making it the superpower it is today." He noted that museum bills had previously passed the House and the Senate, but in different sessions of Congress, and that it was time for both chambers to pass a bill and send it to the President so it could become law. Watts argued that it was quite fitting to locate this museum on the Mall, proximate to the site where Rev. Dr. Martin Luther King, Jr. delivered his epic "I Have A Dream" speech. The creation of this museum, he said, would, "help bring America one step closer to fulfilling Dr. King's dream."

Brownback commented that, "you don't see this array of people supporting too many pieces of legislation," and indeed the press conference was quite an improbable assemblage. Senator Hillary Clinton, then a newly-elected Democrat from New York and former First Lady, and Senator Rick Santorum, a conservative Republican from Pennsylvania, both agreed that the passage of this legislation was imperative, and both noted that Brownback had personally visited them to seek their support. Representative Eddie Bernice Johnson, Democrat of Texas and chair of the Congressional Black Caucus (CBC), reported that the CBC was unified behind the bill, and she thanked the bipartisan leadership and the President for their support. Senator John Edwards, first term Democrat from North Carolina, also spoke eloquently in favor of the bill.

The bipartisan bonhomie was so strong that, during the Q&A with reporters about the depth of support for the bill, Watts, knowing full well that President Bush was firmly on board, turned to Clinton and joked, "Senator Clinton, if the Administration doesn't support [the bill], I'll ask for a recount myself." Everyone on the stage burst out in laughter, friends enjoying each other's company and letting bygones be bygones.

It was a spectacular day. Robert Johnson, the founder of Black Entertainment Television, came to lend his support, and I was honored to meet him. Mark Mitchell and the members of the Friends Group were also there in force, and I valued greeting them as well. Several among the Friends Group were relatives or descendants of prominent African Americans, including Judith Turrentine, widow of the renowned jazz saxophonist Stanley Turrentine, and Jim Henson, the great nephew of famed explorer Matthew Henson.

The president of the Friends Group was also there, a man who identified himself as Frederick Douglass IV and the great, great grandson of Frederick Douglass. With his beard, natty suit, and fedora, this gregarious gentleman evoked the famed abolitionist, and I always enjoyed my conversations with him. While no one I knew questioned his claim at the time, the *Washington Post* later reported that he had been unable to produce documentation corroborating his genealogical claims to Douglass repositories at the National Park Service, Howard University, or the Frederick Douglass Museum and Cultural Center, that some aspects of his story were contradicted by Fred's own father and by documentation found by the *Post*, and that some documented descendants of Frederick Douglass called him "Fake Fred."[4] Whether or not Fred was truly a scion of the great 19th century historical figure, as he continues to maintain, he was certainly a witness to history on that momentous day.

On a Tuesday morning just four months later, everything would change for all present at the sunny press conference. Cleland, a member of the Senate Armed Services Committee, was in the midst of an early morning meeting with the Joint Chiefs of Staff, and Donni Turner, his staff member, was preparing the Senator's briefing materials for a hearing later that day. Suddenly, aides to the Joint Chiefs interrupted and rushed the generals and admirals out of the Senator's office. A plane had just struck one of the twin towers of the World Trade Center in New York City.

Soon after, Capitol Police came to take Cleland, together with all other Senators and the Vice President, to secure locations. The staff was informed that all hearings and official business were cancelled, and individual staffers scattered. As they scrambled hither and yon across the Mall, they learned that a second plane had hit the other Twin Tower, and they could see the smoke in the distance bellowing from the Pentagon.

I, too, remember the horror of that day, because I worried for Amina, who worked a few blocks from the White House, and for my best friend, Melvin Williams, who worked in the World Trade Complex. Fortunately, Amina was able to get safely home, but as I watched the news coverage of people jumping out of windows and the collapsing Twin Towers, all I could do was pray. I did not know which building housed Melvin's office, and I was unable to get word that he was safe until late that afternoon.

This horrific day changed our country's priorities and the congressional outlook toward the museum project. Congress now focused on a war resolution, the USA Patriot Act, and the creation of a new Department of Homeland Security, in addition to the launch of an investigation into what went wrong in preventing the 9/11 attacks.

To top things off, the terrorist attacks had a significant economic impact, generating congressional hesitance to spend money while the economy suffered. Even though the House bill had well over two-hundred co-sponsors and plenty of support to ensure passage, and the Senate bill was supported by most of the key leadership, the seeds of doubt about the potential cost to create the museum, particularly with respect to refurbishing the Arts and Industries Building, began to take root.

Everyone sprang into action. I asked Marshall Purnell, the architect, to help me review various cost estimates, architectural plans, and engineering studies of the Arts and Industries Building. I reviewed our findings with the staff of the Four Musketeers, and we agreed that I should seek a meeting with Secretary Small and Undersecretary Burke to try to pin them down on the amount of, and basis for, the cost estimates that the Smithsonian staff members were feeding Congress. Small agreed to the meeting.

Prior to October 16, 2001, I had never been in the Secretary's suite within the Smithsonian Castle. Like Congressman Lewis's office, it was full of artifacts, but rather than commemorating the Civil Rights movement, these were from all time periods and from all fields of endeavor. While waiting, I gazed at the paintings, sculptures, rare books, and other historical pieces adorning the anteroom. A stuffed leopard, poised as if ready to pounce, stood across from me in the corner, looking much too realistic for my comfort. As I got up to enter Small's office, I pondered whether I was predator or prey, and I felt even more grateful to have Purnell there as backup.

Unfortunately, the crazy events of that time had forced Hilary Shelton to cancel on our meeting. Shelton led congressional relations for the national NAACP, and I knew him from my prior advocacy against racial profiling. He had agreed to join me to share the views of the NAACP with the Smithsonian, but because of his frequent visits to Congress and the mailings of anthrax-filled envelopes to Senate offices, he was due at the doctor for an anthrax test as a precaution.

Nonetheless, Purnell and I had a productive, if sometimes contentious, meeting with Small and Burke. Ultimately, they agreed to what I believed were realistic cost estimates for the Arts and Industries Building. Additionally, they both said they could support the legislation as it had been tweaked by staff.

No matter how much anyone in Congress wants to do something, if the proposal does not have the support of the appropriations committee responsible for its funding, that proposal will never get approved. No one wants to create something that will simply die on the vine. And so it was, in the fall of 2001, when Lewis and Watts found themselves in a fateful meeting with Congressman Ralph Regula, Republican of Ohio and chairman of the appropriations subcommittee vital to the museum bill. Regula was doubly important because he was also a member of the Smithsonian Board of Regents.

In that meeting, Lewis and Watts learned that the détente with Small was too little too late. The damage had already been done. Regula insisted that the museum proposal needed more study, and he pressed Lewis and Watts to agree to move forward in two steps. Congress would create a commission to study the various issues, and Regula promised to fund it. Regula committed that so long as the commission reported to Congress with a workable plan, Regula would support the museum's establishment and funding.

Backed into a corner by a person who held the purse strings, and also served as a Regent on the Smithsonian's governing body, Lewis and Watts had no choice but to agree. A similar meeting took place not long thereafter, this time between the key Senate and House appropriators and Lewis, Watts, Brownback, and Cleland. Tom Downs, a lobbyist with the powerhouse law firm Patton Boggs who represented the Friends Group, sat outside with the staff while those in session ironed out the details of the compromise.

At the conclusion of the meeting, everyone stood to shake hands and convey their congratulations, particularly to Lewis, who had led the struggle for this museum for a decade. Downs looked into the room and saw a particularly poignant scene: Senator Robert Byrd, Democrat of West Virginia and chair of the Senate appropriations committee, a White man who had belonged to the Ku Klux Klan as a young person in the 1940's before renouncing the organization, stood locked in an embrace with Lewis, congratulating him and vowing to support the museum commission. I regret that no one was able to capture that image because, in sharp contrast to the photo of the lynching that Lewis and Brownback had contemplated when they first met to forge their alliance, this picture truly would have been worthy of a postcard.

I confess that I viewed this compromise with great trepidation. Over the prior eight decades, there already had been at least four commissions to study whether and how to create a national African American museum. And still there was no museum.

Hoping to achieve a better outcome, I dug in and worked with staff members to write the strongest bill possible. If we were going to settle for a commission, it would have to be one with some teeth. A bill was drafted to create the National Museum of African American History and Culture Plan for Action Presidential Commission, named as such because it would create a *plan of action* detailing how to move forward. Rather than a commission to draft a report with vague recommendations that ultimately sat on a shelf and gathered dust, this was a commission tasked with writing an actionable plan, with the expectation that, if the members performed and returned with a sound strategy, it would be implemented. That was the only way I was willing to take part.

I was pleased with this outcome, particularly since, as before, my organization was named in the bill—this time as a potential source from which to appoint a member of the Presidential Commission.

The appropriators and congressional leaders kept the first half of the bargain. On December 11, Mr. Lewis, with Watts and Regula as co-sponsors, introduced the Presidential Commission bill.[5] As members of the majority party, Watts or Regula could have laid claim to sponsorship of the bill, but in the bipartisan spirit that permeated this venture, they deferred to Lewis, the longest champion of the issue. The bill bypassed all committees and passed the full House on the same day. The House bill was then sent to the Senate, where it passed the full Senate by unanimous consent on December 17.

For the Congress, this constituted action at warp speed, highly unusual except for urgent, non-controversial legislation. To me, these actions were again symbolic of the support for the idea and the intent to keep the momentum going. This belief was confirmed when President Bush signed the bill into law on December 28th.

A year earlier at this time, I felt like I was barely standing. Now, I was on cloud nine, especially when Mr. Lewis wrote the Speaker of the House to recommend that I, along with Claudine Brown and Lerone Bennett, Jr., be appointed to the Presidential Commission. The train was moving forward, and it appeared that I would not only be on it, but helping to drive. Perhaps I wasn't the prey after all.

My wife, who had devoted so much to this undertaking, shared my elation. She also suggested that perhaps it was time for me to get a job.

CHAPTER NINE

★

A GREAT COMMISSION

On Opening Day 1974, I sat in the stands of Riverfront Stadium, watching the Cincinnati Reds take on the Atlanta Braves. The place was electric, not just because it was the first game of the season, but also because Hank Aaron was poised to tie Babe Ruth's 714 career home run record. This record, held by a baseball legend, was once thought untouchable. And yet, Hammerin' Hank was one swing away from tying it, and one *more* swing from surpassing it. Doing so would be an incredible accomplishment, especially for a player who left the segregated Negro Leagues to join a Major League team.

On his very first at bat, Aaron crushed a Jack Billingham pitch over the left-center field wall. As the crowd erupted, my ten-year-old eyes grew big as saucers. Aaron had tied the Babe! The game halted as the Atlanta bench cleared and Aaron's teammates rushed to congratulate him, soon joined by various baseball officials. Even Vice President Gerald R. Ford came onto the field to mark the occasion. I was a witness to history, and from that moment I was an Aaron fan for life. A few days later, Aaron broke Ruth's record at his home field in Atlanta. My mom bought me a "Hank Aaron 715" baseball glove, which instantly became one of my most cherished possessions.

Not surprisingly, I could barely contain myself when I received the list of appointments to the Presidential Commission and saw the name Henry L. Aaron. I was about to work side-by-side on this epic project with my childhood hero, a baseball Hall of Famer and an important figure in African American history. My precious Hank Aaron glove had gotten lost a few years earlier at an office softball game, but I would soon have a much more significant connection to this legend.

Hank Aaron may have been the most famous, but there were many other prominent members of the commission. I was thrilled to see Cecily Tyson on the list. To me, based upon her award-winning performance in *The Autobiography of Miss Jane Pittman* and her body of work throughout her career, she was a personification of grace and accomplishment, a living embodiment of African American history.

The list contained three members of the Smithsonian's 1990-91 Institutional Study Committee: Claudine Brown, who had chaired that committee, Lerone Bennett Jr. and Howard Dodson. We would greatly benefit from their institutional memory and expertise.

Several appointees held backgrounds in history or museum administration, including Currie Ballard, a professor at Langston University in Oklahoma; Dr. John E. Fleming, the Founding Director of the National Afro-American Museum and Cultural Center in Wilberforce; Barbara Franco, President of the Historical Society of the District of Columbia; and Dr. Harold K. Skramstad, Jr., a former professor and Smithsonian official.

I was also pleased that the list included several appointees with valuable backgrounds in business, management, the media, and civic engagement: Renee' Amoore, a Pennsylvania businesswoman; Vicky Bailey, a business executive and former Assistant Secretary of Energy; Robert W. Bogle, publisher of *The Philadelphia Tribune*, the nation's oldest African American newspaper; Dr. Michael L. Lomax, the President of Dillard University in New Orleans; Andrew G. McLemore, Jr., an executive in a Detroit construction firm; Dr. Eric L. Sexton, an administrator at Wichita State University; Beverly Caruthers Thompson, a retired Topeka, Kansas public school teacher and civic leader, and Dr. Robert L. Wright, the founder and president of a government contracting firm. Congressmen Lewis and Watts, and Senators Brownback and Cleland were designated by Congress as the four nonvoting, ex officio members. This was a diverse and very talented team.

The night before our first meeting—in Washington, where we held all our meetings—we enjoyed a welcome reception and cocktail hour. The atmosphere was exciting, electric, and fired by the feeling of purpose and possibility. A few introductory speeches were made, and then the next day we went to work.

Though our four ex-officio commissioners were busy members of Congress, they joined us to give us our charge. Each spoke briefly but passionately, reiterating the message that we were stewards of a great opportunity. They stressed the importance of the museum, and reminded us how close we were to finally making this project happen after so many years. Their words endowed us with a sense of camaraderie and purpose and got us off to a very inspiring start.

Though I had never met Dr. Wright before beginning this process, I liked and trusted him immediately. An optician by education and training, he had worked in the Small Business Administration during the Reagan Administration. Later, he started a government contracting firm, which he built into a multimillion-dollar company. He brought a tremendous business and organizational background to the commission, as well as very good, long-standing relationships with both Democrats and Republicans on the Hill. On top of all of that, he was a consummate gentleman. Everyone felt he had the leadership ability and the right personality to lead the effort.

By acclamation, we appointed Dr. Wright to be our leader and Claudine Brown to serve as vice chair. They were the perfect team. Dr. Wright, with his political savvy and business experience, was an expert on how to get things done, and Brown had been involved with efforts to create this museum for many years and therefore understood the challenges we faced, including overcoming the concerns of the Smithsonian. The National Museum of African American History and Culture Plan for Action Presidential Commission, by any standard a mouthful, was not going to be a typical "blue-ribbon panel" writing a report that did little more than gather dust. Our commission would be a model of effectiveness.

With our dynamic leadership in place, the Presidential Commission set to work.

Unlike some commissions, created merely to study an issue, we intended to develop and devise an action plan, offering specific steps for moving forward. Dr. Wright wisely recommended that we bring on a project manager to help with the considerable administrative and logistical tasks, which included organizing meetings around the country, drafting our reports, and managing our consultants. A project manager would be critical as we needed to work at a breakneck pace. We brought on Interior Systems, Inc. to handle this part of the mission.

Congress had directed the commission to study and write a report that addressed the museum's governance structure; its location; the availability and cost of collections it would acquire and display; its impact on regional African American museums; and fundraising methods for its creation and maintenance by the American people. Then, we were tasked with incorporating all of that knowledge into a legislative plan of action. To accomplish these myriad tasks, we agreed to organize ourselves into committees. Claudine Brown chaired the committee studying the mission, role, vision, programs, and collection of the museum; Reneé Amoore chaired the legislation and public relations committee; Andrew McLemore Jr. chaired the fundraising, finance and budget committee; Vicky Bailey chaired the governance and organization committee; and I chaired the site and building committee.

Determined to make the most of the momentum in Congress, we put ourselves on a tight timeline. The commission had one year to deliver its report to Congress and the President. Because the members had all been designated by April 1, 2002, we vowed to complete our plan no later than April 2, 2003—even though our first meeting was not until June 2002.

I volunteered to chair the site and building committee. After years of studying the museum efforts, I knew it was going to be one of most difficult and controversial issues we had to tackle. But through my research, I thought I had identified the various arguments that would be made, as well as the best responses to most of them, so I believed that helping to answer the site question was how I could best serve this body.

A major factor in the location study was the museum's relationship with the Smithsonian. If the museum was going to exist within the Smithsonian Institution, the Arts and Industries building was the certain starting point. But did it make sense to use it as a temporary or permanent solution? If temporary, could we find a suitable location for a new building, and if so, would it be on the National Mall? And if the museum was going to be independent of the Smithsonian, our study needed to supply ideas, too.

These were vexing questions. As we faced them, we knew that the consensus among congressional leaders was that the museum should be a part of the Smithsonian: after all, it is the official storyteller and preservationist of the nation. But we also knew that there were doubts within the Smithsonian about its capacity to take on this project.

Questions surrounding location and governance structure were thus both complicated and intertwined. Most of the other issues we were studying overlapped as well, but the committee chairs worked very well together. We collaborated as needed and worked independently when that best moved the ball forward.

To better understand the various governance models, we spoke with numerous Smithsonian officials and worked closely with their staffs. We met with Richard West, the head of the National Museum of the American

Indian, to discuss positives and negatives of that new museum's relationship to the Smithsonian administration, and to solicit any suggestions West could offer as we moved forward in our process. We also met with Earl Powell, director of the National Gallery of Art. The National Gallery, part of the Smithsonian by law, nevertheless runs independently under a board of trustees, an exception demanded by Andrew Mellon, who contributed the initial collection and the money to construct the building. Powell gave us the perspective of a much older and more established institution, as well as one with a large measure of independence.

Ultimately, we concluded that much as we might prefer to have the independent governance of the National Gallery of Art, we were unlikely to gain approval for it from Congress, given that none of the other Smithsonian museums employed that model and the Smithsonian leadership would be vehemently opposed to it. Instead, we agreed upon a governance structure similar to that created for the National Museum of the American Indian, which called for an Advisory Council made up of individuals committed to the museum, who would interact with the Smithsonian Board of Regents to ensure the museum was fairly treated and properly supported and that the director had sufficient independence to do his or her job. That was our recommended compromise.

Determining whether there would be philanthropic support for this museum and what type of public-private partnership to recommend for the funding of the museum was another complex issue. Again, we learned from the approaches taken in the creation of other such museums.

For example, the National Museum of the American Indian, located on the Mall, was originally intended to be built using two-thirds private funds and one-third public funds. In the end, however, about half of the funds came from Congress, and the other half from individuals, corporations, and foundations. The United States Holocaust Memorial Museum, which is not part of the Smithsonian, received federal land and a federal building for free—and receives federal funds every year for planning and administrative support—but almost all of the money to pay for brick-and-mortar construction came from private donors. There were many models, but all required substantial amounts of private funding. As a result, Congress wanted us to confirm that the Black community, and the corporate community in general, would support this huge undertaking.

We were not certain how much money the museum would be able to raise, so we hired consultants, Richard Taft and Alice Green Burnette, to help us answer that question. These experienced fundraisers confidentially surveyed wealthy individuals, foundations, and the corporate community on our behalf, to determine the level of interest in supporting a National Museum of African American History and Culture. The consultants returned with a very positive report, estimating that we could raise approximately $125 million dollars. At that time, we projected the museum would cost roughly $380 million dollars, which meant that we could expect to raise a third of the museum cost from private sources.

We also went to work on a strategic public relations plan. To raise money and implement this project, we needed to create a strong communications platform. We hired Equals Three Communications, a PR firm, to come up with a plan that could be turned over to the museum once the project was authorized. We needed to understand the constituencies that could, and should, be reached, as well as the messages that would energize them. We were guided to think about building a brand and an identity for this museum and finding appropriate partners, especially in the entertainment industry. Stated simply, we needed to figure out how to sell the museum. Lots of great ideas are presented in Washington, D.C., and many of them fail because of the inability to raise sufficient private funds.

As an example, a group of people came together and got approval from Congress in 1984 to create a new memorial on the National Mall to honor Black Revolutionary War patriots.[1] Devroaux and Purnell, the African American architectural firm, and Ed Dwight, an African American sculptor, came up with a beautiful design.[2] Traditionally, money is raised privately to construct memorials; the amount raised has to include an endowment so that funds are available for the National Park Service to maintain the new memorial forever. Despite the powerful concept, a great design, and an ideal location on the Mall, the memorial was never built because the sponsoring group was unable to raise the money.[3]

We did not want the African American museum to meet a similar fate. We wanted to be proactive and create a PR plan that conveyed a sense of urgency in the private sector and reassured Congress that we could sell, and fund, this vision.

Another issue of concern for the commission was the museum's fairly unique circumstance: it did not have a ready-made collection. Typically, when a museum is created, a collection already exists; indeed the collection is usually the raison d'être for the institution. This was the case with several Smithsonian museums, including the National Museum of the American Indian, the Hirshhorn Museum and Sculpture Garden, and the National Museum of African Art.

At the time of our study, the Holocaust Museum was the most prominent major exception to this model. It had been conceived to tell a story about a historical period and a series of events. From there, that museum's organizers went out and assembled the collection and designed the exhibits to tell the story. We were in a similar posture to the Holocaust Museum, but we faced the challenge that, in recent years, no other Smithsonian museum had been formed in this way.

Many skeptics expressed concern about constructing a huge building and then lacking sufficient original and distinguished artifacts to fill it. What if we were unable to find documents, objects, and works of art beyond those already housed in other museums? To explore this issue, we hired experts in collections and their acquisition.

Dr. Deborah Mack and Dr. Gwendolyn Everett surveyed collectors, museums, historically Black colleges and universities, and interested individuals. They discovered lots of people who had been amassing artifacts and art collections. Some were interested in donating items, while others were looking to sell, or perhaps loan, their collections in order to share them with the public. Our survey found that, collectors were waiting for this national museum to arrive. It showed that the museum would indeed be able to build a collection, and that doing so should not be perceived as problematic or unachievable.

Additionally, representatives of smaller African American museums expressed the view that local and regional museums with great historical artifacts would welcome the chance to loan them to a national museum in Washington, D.C., so that millions more people could enjoy them every year. These museums wanted the history to be shared and the common story to be told.

The results were a pleasant surprise, given some of the concerns raised in the past by local and regional African American museums. Many of these museums began in the 1960s, '70s, and '80s, springing up in storefronts or private homes and growing from there. These important establishments existed all over the country, and they wanted the new national museum to complement, rather than detract from, their efforts. As did we.

We hired Joy Ford Austin, the former head of the African American Museums Association and a veteran of the Smithsonian's Institutional Study Committee, to survey local African American museums. She studied the issues and helped us recommend potential solutions. Austin's survey concluded that opposition to a national museum no longer existed. Local museums were onboard and wanted to see the project completed. Their caveat, however, was that they wanted to see it happen in a way that would be beneficial to all.

Based on these findings, the commission recommended that the national museum work with its local counterparts to share collections. Some exhibits could be created and displayed at the national museum and then travel to local museums as well. In that way, the smaller museums would gain access to new content at manageable cost, allowing them to use the new attractions to draw a greater number of visitors. In addition, we recommended a funding stream to allow the smaller institutions to seek federal grants to support their efforts and train their personnel. This made me extremely proud, because the last thing anyone on the commission or in Congress wanted to do was undermine the efforts of these long-standing, and highly important, organizations.

To gauge exactly what the public was interested in seeing in the museum, and to complement and expand upon what already existed in local and regional museums, the commission held town hall meetings in Chicago, New Orleans, New York City, Topeka, Detroit, Washington, and Atlanta. We had hoped to hold them in Dallas, Los Angeles, and Oklahoma City as well, but our budget was tight and we ran out of time. We asked people about stories they wanted to see in relation to the African American experience, as well as which stories they believed had been omitted or misinterpreted that they hoped the museum would correct. We also asked how the museum should reach out and communicate its progress. We hoped the answers would guide curators and museum administrators in their future efforts.

I found the town hall meetings to be well attended and quite compelling. Participants were really excited to hear that the museum might finally happen and to have a voice in its creation. As part of our presentation, we put together a slide show that discussed the history of the efforts to create the museum, the purpose of the commission, biographical information about the members, what we intended to study, and what Congress had asked us to cover in our report. Cicely Tyson helped design and narrate the slide show. It was very special for her to be involved, as she is so well respected, particularly within the African American community. This was one of many ways in which Ms. Tyson, like Mr. Aaron, actively participated in the work of the Commission, rather than just lending a famous name to the cause.

Thanks to these meetings, the commission learned of areas of specific interest within the community, including the Pullman porters and their impact on the development of the Black middle class; the great migration of Blacks from the south to the north in the early 1900s up to the pre-World War II period; the Tuskegee Airmen; and scientists and inventors like Benjamin Banneker.

Additionally, people were very interested in hearing and learning from oral histories, as well as having the opportunity to come to the museum and create oral histories or contribute those of relatives. Participants also discussed the importance of telling the history of slavery and the Jim Crow period, as well as of African American soldiers and sailors and their participation in all of America's wars. The classical arts were mentioned, along with interest in the intersection of African Americans with Native Americans and other people of color, the Underground Railroad, and social and fraternal organizations Blacks created to protect and enjoy their communities. A vast spectrum of topics, to be sure, and the enthusiasm was strong and heartening.

Not surprisingly, most members of the public had no idea how long the process of establishing this museum had been going on, and certainly not that the efforts dated back to 1916. I wanted that knowledge to be at the forefront of everyone's mind. The trial lawyer in me treated this process in much the same way I approached the goal of persuading a jury. I wanted as many people as possible to know about the other commissions that had been formed over the years, and all of the obstacles that had appeared in the path, so that we did not repeat mistakes of the past. My mantra: "Enough already."

I had taken the same approach at the first meeting of the commission. I wrote a report called *The Forgotten Museum*, and I gave a copy to every single commissioner.[4] I wanted everyone to know the long history of this project and how important it was that we succeed in this mission after more than eighty years. I wanted to create a sense of urgency and momentum so that we would finally see this vision through.

Inspired by that urgency, as we approached our deadline, the commission set out to assemble the data and write our final report. The prologue to the report was adapted from *The Forgotten Museum* to ensure that the President and Congress were aware of the museum's long struggle to come into existence. But that was not enough; we wanted to convey the sense of urgency that we all felt and had been expressed by people all over the nation. Thus, we also decided that the report needed a mission statement as part of the introduction. I volunteered to draft it.

I felt honored to be given this important, and daunting, task. The body of the report would, of course, contain all the facts, figures, and analysis, but this mission statement was supposed to explain the significance of where we had come from, what we had done, and why this action plan needed to be implemented. I worked very hard on that statement, and I wrote what I thought was a very powerful draft. I was proud of my work.

Once I finished, a small group of the commission members got together to discuss the statement and to edit it for inclusion in our final report. Suddenly, the gravity of the situation hit me. Three formidable scholars were reading my work and going over every word with a fine-toothed comb. Lerone Bennett Jr. had written several classic texts on African American history, Howard Dodson was the long-time head of one of the most esteemed African American research institutions in the nation, and Dr. Michael Lomax was a university president and a literary scholar in his own right. What had I gotten myself into?

After a period of deathly silence, Bennett told me that the draft was good, but then he asked if I would let him take it and work on it a bit. He said we needed to "sauce it up some," that it had "too much Harvard and not enough Howard." Dodson and Lomax concurred, and they offered other observations and suggestions. My heart sank. I thought I had really knocked it out of the park like my hero Mr. Aaron, but it seemed that the group thought it was more like a long single. Then I remembered that, as with anything else, you can do good work on your own, but a team can make much more. I accepted Bennett's suggestion to set to work on the piece.

Impeccably dressed as usual in a three-piece suit, Bennett took off his jacket, rolled up his shirt sleeves, and headed off to do his part. He emerged from his hotel room a couple hours later with a reworked, and beautiful, mission statement that became part of our final document. He wrote the line, 'The Time Has Come,' which expressed our collective sense and became the report title. We worked late into the night, poring over every word as we finalized the language.

That interaction was special. I so enjoyed being part of the creative process with people of their stature. It was a powerful thing to synthesize and express the emotions of the commission, to explain what we did, why it was important, and why Congress and the President needed to act on our recommendations. Bringing our thoughts together in this way proved to be a great climax to the whole experience.

But that night was one of multiple highly memorable events in our work. The camaraderie and shared sense of urgency had driven us throughout. We did not have time for a 'my way or the highway' approach. We would respectfully debate an issue, and then move toward consensus and compromise. Each commission member chose to minimize his or her self in order to maximize the group, and that choice made all the difference.

The result of our collaboration on the mission statement is as follows:

The National Museum of African American History and Culture will give a voice to the centrality of the African American experience and will make it possible for all people to understand the depths, complexity, and promise of the American experience. The museum will serve as a national forum for collaboration with educational and cultural institutions in the continuing quest for freedom, truth, and human dignity.[5]

Thus, we concluded that we should have this separate museum, but that it shouldn't just be seen as a Black history museum. Rather, it should be seen as a museum intended to help the visitor better understand American history through the lens of Black history, which offers a unique view of the country and its development. For instance, one cannot properly understand the U.S. Constitution without studying how slavery affected the provisions dealing with the voting structure of the Congress and the relationship between the federal government and the states, as well as how the fight against slavery led to constitutional amendments to end slavery and to give full citizenship and voting rights to African Americans. In addition, we believed that, while this museum would have a stage on a national forum, it would also collaborate with other institutions within the Smithsonian, local and regional African American museums, and other mainstream American museums, fostering a dialogue all over the country.

We lived up to our name as a *plan for action* Presidential Commission, and our year-long journey yielded a real plan, and one of great value. It was an amazing experience that I will cherish until my dying days, even more than that baseball glove.

CHAPTER TEN

★

LOCATION, LOCATION, LOCATION

Of all the issues to be resolved in creating a national African American history museum, location—a hornet's nest of politics, dueling federal agencies, celebrity sensibilities, and regulatory mayhem—proved to be the most controversial. Because I knew that disputes over location, to a large degree, had killed the project when it had its best chance of passing the Congress in 1992, I volunteered to chair the site and building committee of the Presidential Commission.

Our congressional sponsors wanted this museum on the National Mall and the location had the potential to be the biggest stumbling block to consensus so, as chair of the Presidential Commission's site and building committee, I was determined that we put forward the best arguments for a Mall site. I had painstakingly researched past arguments, pro and con, and the histories of other Mall museums, so I came to the committee armed and ready to serve. With more than a decade of experience as a trial lawyer, I thought of this as the trial of my lifetime, one in which I would literally have to build a monumental case.

The first factor making site selection so complex was symbolism, particularly as related to the unique nature of the National Mall. The Mall was a finite space sought out by a seemingly infinite number of ideas and proposals for monuments, memorials and museums. In a perfect world, the Mall would have room for every appropriate use, but limited real estate requires difficult choices. We have always had to plan carefully for what could be located on the Mall, and how the overall space is best used.

When the District of Columbia was designed to be the nation's capital, President George Washington tasked planner Pierre L'Enfant with laying out the city. L'Enfant was aided by Benjamin Banneker, an African American surveyor. Together, the two devised the concept of the National Mall running across the center of the city (figure 3).

The L'Enfant Plan was revisited in 1901 at the behest of Senator James McMillan, who sponsored a commission to update the plan composed of Daniel Burnham, Frederick Law Olmsted, Jr., and Charles McKim. The new plan, when finished, was called the McMillan Plan, after the Michigan Senator (figure 4).

The McMillan Plan reserved the area along the National Mall for museums and monumental buildings. There were other facilities along the Mall at the time, including a railroad, a hotel, a restaurant, and row houses. Those structures were eventually torn down to beautify the city and make the Mall area available for its purpose according to the plan.

Then, in 1910, Congress created the Commission on Fine Arts (CFA) as an independent agency to review the design of anything constructed in the area of the National Mall, including office buildings, monuments, memorials, and museums.[1] Reflecting the influence of the McMillan Plan, both Burnham and Olmstead were appointed to this new body, with Burnham serving as its first chairman.[2]

The development of the Mall has been jealously guarded ever since. Another entity, the National Capital Planning Commission (NCPC), was created to oversee planning of the nation's capital and to review construction projects throughout the city, but especially in the area of the National Mall. As a result, the CFA, NCPC, the National Park Service, and various other agencies and advisory boards review all aspects of design for anything located on the National Mall or near national monuments. An alphabet soup of entities must be involved with any construction on or near the Mall.

Lying beneath all of these jurisdictions and regulations was the notion of priority. What was important enough for inclusion? What deserved to represent and honor our nation on the National Mall? These questions will forever be embedded in the scrutiny of any proposal for any museum, monument, or memorial. And that issue was magnified, in symbolism, history, and a myriad of other ways, when the discussion involved an African American museum.

The 1968 proposal to create a national African American history museum in Wilberforce, Ohio, was tied to that community's history as an Underground Railroad stop and a settlement of freed slaves, but the proposal failed to move forward on a federal level. The next big push for a national institution, this time to be located in Washington, D.C., was in the 1980s.

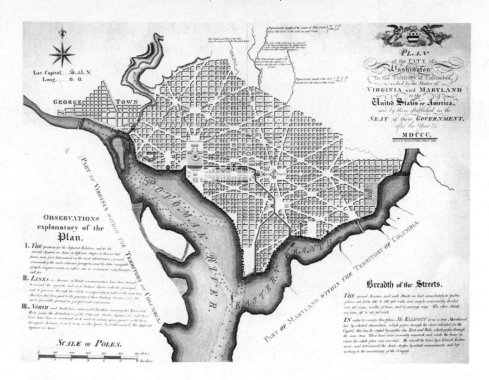

Figure 3. 1791 L'Enfant Plan[3]

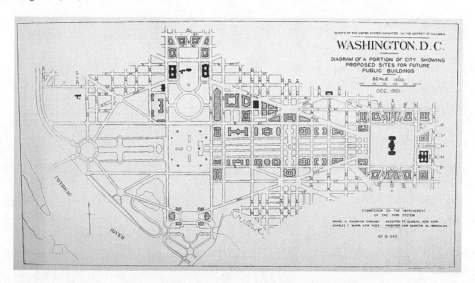

Figure 4. The 1901 McMillan Plan diagram of the National Mall[4]

That proposal introduced the idea of using an existing facility for the museum, the Arts and Industries Building next to the Smithsonian Castle.

Originally built as a temporary structure to house exhibitions from the Centennial World's Fair of 1876, the Arts and Industries Building was the first museum building constructed by the Smithsonian, opening in 1881.[5] Although a handsome structure, the building leaked like a sieve, primarily because it was never intended to be permanent. Smithsonian Secretary S. P. Langley described the edifice as a "cheap," "expedient," and "temporary" exhibition space and sought funds to replace it in the early 1900s,[6] and the McMillan Plan called it "inadequate and unsuited" for its purpose and recommended its replacement.[7] Despite the criticism, this "temporary" structure dodged the wrecking ball in the ensuing decades, and in 1971 it was designated a National Historic Landmark precisely because it had survived. It is one of the best-preserved examples of the 19th century "world's fair" or "exposition" architectural style of buildings.

Though historically significant, the Arts and Industries Building is something of a white elephant on the National Mall. It was designed to be a museum at a time when the requirements for museums, and even the concept of a museum itself, differed greatly from current requirements and schools of thought. The building was not built to have the proper temperature and humidity controls necessary for a modern museum exhibit space, presenting difficult engineering and design challenges for use holding priceless and delicate artifacts.

The Arts and Industries Building was also problematic because it was relatively small compared to other museums, between 150,000 and 175,000 square feet, depending upon the method of measurement. The United States Memorial Holocaust Museum, for example, has more than 300,000 square feet in two buildings, and the National Museum of the American Indian was planned for approximately 400,000 square feet. In theory, renovation was possible, including underground excavation to add basement space. But even speaking abstractly, that was a complex and expensive solution.

At any rate, in the 1980s, the path of least resistance and the easiest way to gain a location on the National Mall was to make use of the Arts and Industries Building. By 1992, the leadership of the Smithsonian got behind that plan but, as described earlier, some critics found the suggestion of the Arts and Industries Building unacceptable given its many limitations. Museum supporters had been unable to compromise and get everyone behind the Arts and Industries Building, and no legislative proposal could pass both the House and Senate in the same two-year Congress to have a chance of becoming law. Because of the dissent over location, the Arts and Industries Building's use even a temporary solution had not been approved.

Now, ten years later, we were in largely the same place, and I dedicated myself to making sure location would not be a barrier once again.

In addition to the government actors, I knew that the commission's work would interest an organization called the National Coalition to Save Our Mall, led by Judy Scott Feldman. This group believed that the Mall area was overbuilt, that no other structures should be allowed, and that the Mall itself should be protected as a no-build zone. In the 1990s, the Coalition tried to block the placement of the World War II memorial between the Washington Monument and the Lincoln Memorial. It even sued the government in an attempt to keep the memorial project from going forward. In response, Congress passed a law ratifying the placement of the memorial at that site and declaring that no federal courts could hear any lawsuits on the issue,[8] which put an end to the formal opposition but also caused a good deal of bitterness among these devotees of Mall preservation.

In an effort to prevent what they considered to be future mistakes, the NCPC—with the support of the CFA, the National Park Service, the Coalition, and others—worked in the late 1990s to create a master plan for memorials and museums. Significantly, the NCPC plan established an area called "The Reserve," a no-build zone at the core of the Mall. Additionally, the plan encouraged placement of future monuments and memorials nearby but outside of the Mall area, as well as in other parts of the city, with the hope of expanding the vision of the Mall so that more locations would be considered acceptable and important. These specifications applied to new museums, too.

Prior to my formal involvement with the commission, also in the late 1990s, I sought a meeting with Judy Scott Feldman. I wanted to talk to her about the African American museum and seek support and assistance from her and her organization in trying to help us find a location on the Mall. While the meeting was cordial, we had to agree to disagree on the issue. So, despite my determination to avoid past sticking points, I knew that these organizations—the National Coalition to Save Our Mall, the National Park Service, and the National Capital Planning Commission—were not going to support placing a national African American museum in a new building on the Mall. We had a fight on our hands.

As Congressman Lewis had expressed at the press conference in 2001, a big part of the African American story is overcoming the requirement of coming in through the back door or having to use a separate entrance. The National Mall is America's front lawn, Congressman Lewis stressed. Black Americans should be able to enter onto the front lawn and have a place there. As a nation, it would serve as a very powerful symbol of how far things have progressed for this museum to be on that front lawn instead of off to the side, someplace seen and not heard.

Congressman Lewis's sentiment was echoed in town hall meetings, surveys, and focus group sessions conducted by the Presidential Commission. The American people, Black and White, agreed with his argument that a location on the Mall would be a meaningful token to counter that unfortunate part of America's history that denied citizenship to people of African descent and relied on them to support, enrich, and serve the nation while denying their humanity. The average person on the street understood the problematic symbolism of locating this museum off the Mall, given the history of subjugation.

As a practical concern, our research had also revealed that donor interest was much higher for a museum located on the Mall rather than in an alternate location. Given that we had to raise a substantial amount of private funds to support this museum, and that donors were likely to give more enthusiastically and generously to an institution showcased on the 'front lawn,' it seemed prudent to incorporate their preference into our action plan.

Despite the commission's leanings, we could not ignore the fact that Congress had directed us to study the Arts and Industries Building to determine the feasibility of its use. We called in architects and planners to help us assess the necessary temperature and humidity controls, as well as the possibility of building an underground annex. We discussed whether the exhibits that needed temperature and humidity controls could be located down, with other types of exhibits and uses not requiring strict temperature and humidity controls placed above ground.

After many such discussions, we came up with a design, which ultimately led to the conclusion that it would cost more to repurpose that building and expand it than it would to construct a new building, regardless of site location.

As in all things, cost was an issue, both the cost to the American people through appropriated funds and to the community through those raised privately. We also determined that new construction, designed specifically for this project, would allow the structure itself to be part of the story. Museums, in particular, are often designed to make use of elements like shape, color, texture, and size to add to the larger narrative and enrich the overall experience. This effect would not be possible if we were tied to the existing Arts and Industries Building.

All this led us to one important question: Was there an appropriate spot on the Mall for this museum? I believed so. As chair of the site and building committee, it was my job to educate the rest of the commission, and I pointed them to what I had discovered about the L'Enfant design plan for Washington, D.C.

When created in 1791, the L'Enfant Plan placed squares along the Mall, noting locations considered appropriate for museums. Low and behold, between our current 14th and 15th Streets and south of what is now Constitution Avenue, Northwest, the plan called for a museum building on that site. The McMillan Plan of 1901 did the same (figures 5 and 6).

At first, I assumed this information would simplify a complex issue, but that was not the case. Those in favor of limiting construction on the Mall dismissed those plans as outdated and referenced what they termed a

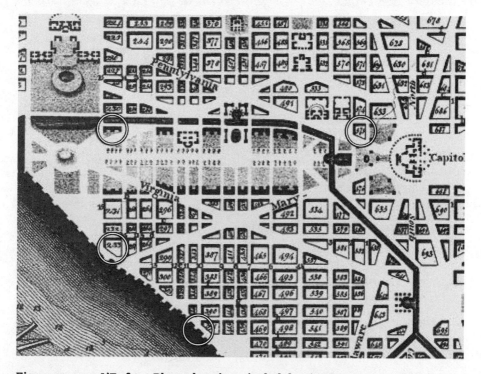

Figure 5. 1791 L'Enfant Plan, showing circled, beginning at top left and proceeding clockwise: the site at 14th Street and Constitution Avenue, the site at 3rd Street and Constitution Avenue, the site at Banneker Overlook, and the site of the Liberty Loan Building.[9]

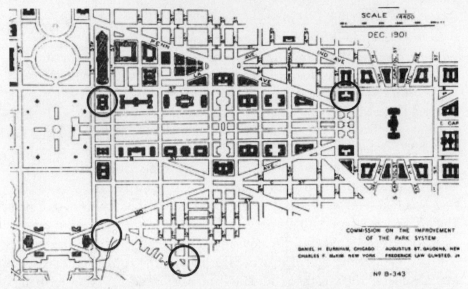

Figure 6. 1901 McMillan Plan, showing circled, beginning at top left and proceeding clockwise: the site at 14th Street and Constitution Avenue, the site at 3rd Street and Constitution Avenue, the site at Banneker Overlook, and the site of the Liberty Loan Building.[10]

'current plan,' approved by the National Capital Planning Commission in 1966. That plan does not show a building between 14th and 15th Streets and south of Constitution Avenue. Rather, it shows green space there.

So I did more homework. I studied the 1966 plan (figure 7) and the records of the various planning agencies and learned that when the Smithsonian sought to build the Hirshhorn Museum on the Mall, that museum was approved and built despite the fact that the 1966 plan indicated no building should be placed there. Similarly, the east wing of the National Gallery of Art was built in the late 1970s on a location that, according to the 1966 Mall master plan, should remain green space. The same was true for the new buildings constructed for the United States Memorial Holocaust Museum and the National Museum of the American Indian. And all of this was done with the blessing of the NCPC.

In light of this, I argued that the 1966 master plan was far from sacrosanct. If the goal was to preserve the Mall according to the intentions of the city founders and planners, then the plans created in 1791 and 1901 were the more authentic and appropriate choices, more closely aligned with the original vision for Washington, D.C. In addition, if there was some reason why the 1966 plan should take precedence, then that should be explained,

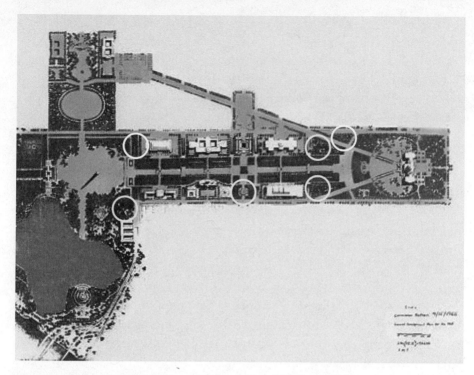

Figure 7. 1966 NCPC Mall Master Plan, showing circled, across the top beginning on the left: the proposed site at 14th Street and Constitution Avenue, the site of the East Wing of the National Gallery of Art, the proposed site at 3rd Street and Constitution Avenue; and across the bottom beginning on the left: the site of the Holocaust Museum, the site of the Hirshhorn Museum, the site of National Museum of the American Indian.[11]

as well as how it had been appropriate to make exceptions for four different museums in the preceding decades, but not to make the same exception now for the African American museum.

The history was front of mind to the members of the Presidential Commission, including me. It was not lost on us that in 1929 Congress had previously created a commission to plan, raise money for, and build this very museum, then called the National Memorial Building to Negro Achievement and Contributions to America. Due to opposition from southern Democratic congressmen, not a penny was spent at that time, and then the Great Depression hit, which kept the project from ever getting off the ground.

Based on that history, my argument—one fully supported by the Presidential Commission—was that our museum was grandfathered. While we could understand making a case for keeping some other museum off the

Mall, if any museum merited exceptional treatment, it was this one. This institution should have been built generations earlier, but for racial opposition, bureaucratic indifference, and unforeseeable national tragedy.

Our opposition did not see things the same way. We were going to have to go up against planning bodies that fixed on the 1966 master plan and the notion that the Mall could not handle one more museum.

The NCPC approved "The Reserve." Based on that new plan, the no-build zone on the Mall included the site between 14th and 15th Streets near the Washington Monument and it provided that nothing—not a statue, not a memorial, and definitely not a building—should ever be placed in that area. Legislation was introduced to turn these recommendations into law, which would have meant the end of our efforts to place our museum on the Mall, at least absent a legislative exception.

There was a strong push to pass the bill creating The Reserve at the same time our commission toiled to complete our action plan and recommendations with the competing goal to obtain congressional approval for a new museum on the Mall. Fortunately, LaRochelle Young of Senator Brownback's staff kept an eye on all of this, and Brownback placed a hold on the bill creating The Reserve. Once Brownback received assurances that the National Museum of African American History and Culture would be exempted from The Reserve, the hold was lifted and the bill eventually passed, but our museum stood safely out of its reach.[12]

At one of the commission's meetings to discuss location choices, we heard from John Parsons, the National Park Service official with oversight of the Mall and a member of the National Capital Planning Commission. Parsons suggested that we would be crazy to push for a site on the Mall since Congress would disapprove it, the planning commissions would reject it, and the National Park Service would oppose it.

Parsons recommended that we consider a location off the Mall in an area near the wharf and the marina known as Banneker Overlook, the location preferred for our project by the Park Service and the NCPC. He stressed that there would be no bureaucratic opposition to this selection; just the opposite, in fact. He also pointed out that the site overlooked the water, which allowed for the possibility of incorporating a slave ship element into the design. The site was relatively large, nearly eight acres, compared to the five-acre site near the Washington Monument.

The NCPC and the Park Service also pointed to the fact that other new museums would invariably be built in the vicinity in the future, and thus, because the waterfront area was going to undergo major redevelopment, our museum could help promote those efforts in that part of the city. It could also spur new thinking about how museums located away from the Mall could be successful tourist destinations. We were told that our project would be a trailblazer at the forefront of this new line of thought.

While those suggestions were legitimate pros, ultimately the commission didn't believe they were sufficient to outweigh the potential cons: lower visitation, lower interest in the project by the private donor community, and the lost opportunity for the innate symbolism of locating this particular museum "in America's front yard," rather than in the rear or off to the side. An important part of our mission was to educate the country about African American history as part of all our history, and we believed that this museum would more effectively accomplish that mission in a location where people who might not have planned to visit it happen to stumble upon it and decide to see what it is about. We did not want the museum be a place where only Blacks, or others with a pre-developed interest in African American history, would go. Given a Mall location, Americans, and even international tourists, who were not necessarily coming to Washington to learn about African American history, might feel inspired to come inside and discover something new.

We struggled on, despite continuing pushback. Notwithstanding our arguments based on the L'Enfant and McMillan plans, critics argued that while buildings had been drawn at certain locations, construction did not occur, which made those drawings conceptual rather than portraying sites for serious consideration.

So I did more research, and it paid off. While perusing the annals of the Library of Congress, I learned that, in the exact same location as the site between 14th and 15th Streets south of Constitution Avenue, government officials had planned in the early 20th century to build a new headquarters for the State Department. While the construction eventually took place a couple of miles away, in Foggy Bottom, the approval on our target site was new history to me. I dug further and found design plans for the building—in a large, neoclassical style popular at that time—that the CFA had formally approved in 1911. Recall that Congress had even appointed two of the three main architects of the McMillan Plan, Daniel Burnham and Frederick Law Olmsted, to the Commission on Fine Arts, so they were part of the approval.

The discovery was huge. I had seen that to the planning community, the L'Enfant Plan was treated as the Old Testament, so to speak, and the McMillan Plan the New Testament. Together, they made up the Bible of the

National Mall. My research had revealed that the "New Testament" authors had blessed a building on our target site on the Mall. It was game changing. I thought the 1911 approval of the State Department building destroyed any historical, intellectual, or design-based arguments against building our museum there.

At this point, we had a very compelling case for the site near the Washington Monument, but I and the other members of the commission knew that the National Park Service, the NCPC, and others would still be against it, notwithstanding the mountain of evidence. So we set our sights on another location at the opposite end of the National Mall, toward the U.S. Capitol. The east wing of the National Gallery of Art occupied the space between Third and Fourth Streets, at Constitution Avenue. Directly adjacent, an empty piece of land sat between First and Third Streets.

According to both the L'Enfant and McMillan plans, a building was designated to occupy this empty site. In fact, buildings had once been located there—not monumental buildings but row houses and a boarding house—but they were razed long ago, leaving this area green space for the past several decades. We thought we could put our museum there, as a sister structure to the Botanic Garden building on the other side of the Mall, across the Capitol reflecting pool.

It certainly was a worthy location, but there was a bureaucratic aspect to it that seemed especially favorable. The site is on what is legally the Capitol Grounds, which meant that Congress, through the office of the Architect of the Capitol, had direct administrative responsibility for the terrain and any construction and operation on it, not the National Park Service. Physically, it is part of the National Mall, but legally, it is not. The advantage of what we on the commission began to call the 'Capitol site' was that, if Congress approved of us putting a museum there, the NCPC would have no formal say. The National Park Service and the CFA would have some input on design aspects of the building, but not on whether a building should go in that location.

The Capitol site was about the same size as the site near the Washington Monument, which added to its appeal. We met with the Architect of the Capitol, and he did not indicate any opposition—in fact, he seemed supportive, and we thought we would be able to build support in Congress for this location. This site, and the site near the Washington Monument, which we called the "Monument site," emerged as our two best choices for putting the museum in a newly constructed building on the Mall.

To be thorough, we studied other sites near the Mall, ultimately producing a shortlist of the five best potential locations. These top contenders were the Banneker Overlook site, near the water; the Monument site; the Capitol site; the Arts and Industries Building, located next to Smithsonian Castle; and a location we referred to as the Liberty Loan site.

Situated at the end of 14th Street and close to the Tidal Basin, along which the Jefferson and the Martin Luther King, Jr. memorials sit, the Liberty Loan site was occupied by a building with no historical significance constructed during World War II and intended to be temporary. Our commission, based on input from the planning officials, reasoned that it could be torn down without historical consequences to make way for the museum. Here, the museum would be near significant memorials, the Tidal Basin, and the cherry blossoms so many visitors come to see in the spring.

Though the Liberty Loan site was, technically, not on the Mall, it was situated just two blocks away, with only the United States Memorial Holocaust Museum and a couple of government buildings separating it. It was, however, a small site, with few options for landscaping or an outdoor plaza, and no possibility of future expansion. Despite its problematic aspects, the site offered enough positive attributes to be included in our top five.

This list of the five had been culled, through intense brain and foot work, from a larger group of eleven possible locations. The commission had hired E. Verner Johnson and Associates, architects and museum planners, to evaluate all the sites, as well as to determine, and instruct us in, the criteria we should use to rank them. To determine these final five, the entire commission took a field trip and toured the original eleven sites so that we could fully consider them.

That was a thrilling day. We hired a charter bus and filled it with the commissioners, the congressional staff members and the consultants. Two U.S. Park Police motorcycle officers, both of whom happened to be African American, escorted us, sirens wailing, so we could cut through traffic and reach all the intended sites in a day. Although I had never had the privilege of traveling in a presidential motorcade, I felt the thrill of that symbol of public urgency as we avoided all traffic and ran through red lights to complete our mission that day.

Our brawny police escorts were particularly impressive, and they clearly enjoyed escorting dignitaries and being part of our mission. It was a treat to watch them handle their Harley-Davidsons with such skill, sometimes riding with no hands as they motioned to passersby and directed traffic along the way. As the outing organizer, I took special pride in the fun we were able to have as we carried out our work.

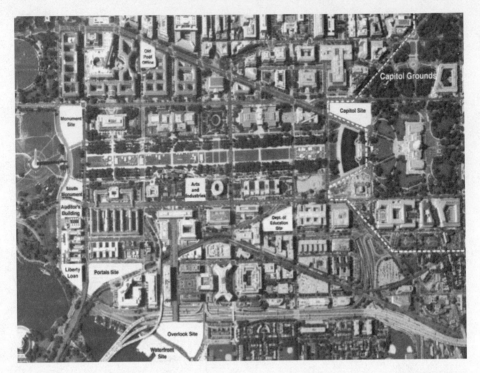

Figure 8. Aerial Photo depicting all eleven of the sites evaluated by the Presidential Commission[13]

At each of the eleven locations, our consultants briefed us on what they considered its pros and cons. Commissioners walked around, asked questions, and generally developed an opinion with regard to each location. After the tour, we voted, with the goal of whittling the list down to a more manageable number. From that group, we voted on our first choice, allowing our final report to designate a single desired location and explain why we considered it the best option.

We chose the Capitol site for our lead recommendation, though the rankings were very, very close between it and the Monument site, with only two points separating them in our scoring system. While practically a tie, from a political standpoint, the Capitol site seemed more likely to gain approval because of the administrative quirk of control by the Legislative Branch and we had, at that point, encountered less opposition to it than the Monument site.

Accordingly, in our final report, the Presidential Commission recommended that Congress specifically designate the Capitol site as the location for the museum. We also recommended that Congress do so without going through any further deliberation and consultation, just as Congress had designated the specific site for the National Museum of the American Indian, the National Air and Space Museum, and the Hirshhorn Museum. But the planning officials objected to direct designation as circumventing their role, notwithstanding precedents.

Unfortunately, by the time we submitted our final report to Congress in April 2003, two leaders of our 2001 legislative fight had departed from the Congress. Senator Cleland lost his 2002 reelection bid, and Congressman Watts declined to run for reelection to the House in 2002.

Nonetheless, Congressman Lewis and Senator Brownback soldiered on, as driven as ever. They decided that, rather than designating a specific site, they would draft legislation allowing the Smithsonian Board of Regents to select the location from among the top sites identified by the Presidential Commission. However, Lewis, Watts, Brownback, and Cleland had always been opposed to the Banneker Overlook site for this museum, believing that it was too remote from the Mall and that the symbolism in placing this museum at that location would be all wrong. So Lewis and Brownback dropped that option and the bills they introduced provided that the Smithsonian Board of Regents would select the site from among the Arts and Industries Building, the Capitol site, the Monument site, and the Liberty Loan site.

The bills also provided that the Regents should consult with the chair and ranking members of the relevant House and Senate Committees, the chair of the National Capital Planning Commission, the chair of the Commission of Fine Arts, and the museum's Advisory Council. Significantly, the bills also required the Regents to take into consideration the reports and plans of the Presidential Commission, and to consult with the chair, vice chair, and the chair of the site and building committee of the commission. I was gratified to see that the hard work we had done would be considered as the process moved forward.

Initially, things moved quickly. On May 23, 2003, Brownback introduced his bill, and from the Senate floor, he thanked the 45 original cosponsors of the bill and gave special thanks to Senator Chris Dodd (now leading the effort on the Democratic side), and fellow Republicans Ted Stevens and Rick Santorum for their support.[14] On June 24, just a month later, the Senate bill was discharged from the Senate Rules Committee without even a hearing, and it passed the full Senate by unanimous consent on the same day.[15] We were cooking with gas.

But, yet again, complications intervened.

Rather than follow the path of the Senate, the House committee that oversaw the Smithsonian, the Committee on House Administration, decided to hold hearings on Lewis's bill. The hearing was set for July 9, and even though the Senate passage provided some wind to our backs, we sensed the headwinds of opposition. The members of the Presidential Commission remained steadfast in support of the site recommendations, and Dr. Wright and Claudine Brown, our chair and vice chair, appeared at the hearing, accompanied by myself and Howard Dodson. We were determined to see our plan succeed.

The first person to speak at the hearing was Congressman Lewis, the legislative and spiritual leader of our movement. He made a passionate case for the bill, preemptively responding to concerns he had heard and defending the extensive study and work done by the Presidential Commission. Lewis recounted how he started work on the museum fifteen years earlier, saying, "[w]hen we began this journey, I often said that we must pace ourselves for the long haul. Well, we have paced ourselves. We have been patient. The commission has submitted a thorough and complete report. The Senate has acted and passed legislation establishing a national African American museum. Now it is time for the House to do its job."[16] Congressman Jack Kingston, a fellow Georgian who had agreed to take the lead on the Republican side now that Watts had left the House, followed Lewis.

We were wise not to take this hearing for granted, because as soon as Lewis, Kingston and our chair, Dr. Wright, finished their eloquent comments, the advocates of the no-build faction spoke forcefully in opposition to the Capitol site. Charles Cassell, an architect and member of the National Coalition to Save Our Mall, testified that, while the site was not technically part of the National Mall, it was nonetheless symbolically a part of the Mall. To further its aim to stop all building on the Mall, the Coalition asked Congress to put its foot down and make law that nothing more could go on the National Mall, now and forever, precluding any future exceptions. Cassell therefore urged the Committee to remove the Capitol and Monument sites from consideration. He was backed by George Oberlander, another member of the Coalition, who also happened to be a former long-time employee of the NCPC.[17]

Dr. Wright responded to these points and various other questions posed by committee members. Brown and I chimed in to assist as necessary. We explained, for what seemed like the umpteenth time, how the Capitol and Monument sites were consistent with the L'Enfant and McMillan plans and how Congress had specifically designated other Smithsonian museums for Mall sites. Congresswoman Eleanor Holmes Norton, Democrat from the District of Columbia and herself a titan of the Civil Rights Movement, also spoke in our defense, pointing out the flaws in the objections to the Capitol site.

However, there was plenty more opposition. Various Capitol officials appeared after we finished our testimony to express concerns, which revolved around the fact that ours would be a Smithsonian museum, and as such would typically be protected by Smithsonian Police. But, if it were located at the Capitol site, which is protected by the Capitol Police, there would be bureaucratic and jurisdictional issues. Lost in this discussion was the fact that the Supreme Court of the United States is technically situated on Capitol Grounds, but protected by the Supreme Court Police, rather than the Capitol Police, without any great jurisdictional conflict.

Others raised concerns about whether Congress might need the additional space for its own use in the future, and therefore perhaps consideration of the Capitol site should await the completion of further planning about those future needs.[18] Just what we needed; the delay of this project for another study.

Alas, our best laid plans had gone awry. Though the commission thought the Capitol site would offer the greatest chance of reaching consensus, in the end, consensus could not be had. Enough questions were raised that key members of House expressed uncertainty about whether the Capitol site was the best location, or whether it should be considered at all. Unfortunately, the terms of the House bill, as then written, could not gain enough support to move forward.

This was a low point in the process for me. I felt like I had failed the Presidential Commission. I had led the siting effort, and we had studied the issues, considered the arguments, and reached agreement within the commission, but we had not closed the deal with Congress. We convinced many, but not enough. I began to worry that our plan would meet the same fate as all of the prior undertakings to create this museum. It was a nightmare.

As they had been throughout this process, Lewis and Brownback remained unified and undeterred. They worked with the Presidential Commission, other interested parties, and most importantly, the critics in the House, to respond to the various concerns and forge an agreeable compromise. Even though Lewis and Brownback opposed the Banneker Overlook site, they agreed to amend the bill. The Capitol site would be replaced by the Banneker Overlook site. The National Capital Planning Commission urged Congress to narrow the choices even further, so that Regents could choose only between the Arts and Industries Building and the Banneker

Overlook.[19] The Presidential Commission opposed those efforts, and fortunately, Congress was not persuaded to follow that recommendation.

With this amendment, Lewis secured the agreement of the House leadership to move forward, and to do so quickly. Rather than introduce a separate Senate bill, Brownback planned to move Lewis's bill after it passed the full House, hoping that he could get a museum bill through the Senate again, just as he had in June. On November 17, Lewis introduced a new bill with the amended language, and on the very next day, the leadership brought the bill before the full House for a vote.

When Lewis rose to speak, he thanked the many people who had supported the bill, including his colleagues in the House and Senate, all of the staff members, and the Presidential Commission, noting that "[i]t has been a long, hard, and tedious journey." He was clearly gratified that this long deferred dream was on a firm path toward realization. "The African American story must be told, and a National African American Museum in Washington, D.C., is critical to telling that story. African American history is the story of hundreds, thousands, and millions of ordinary men, women, and children struggling to survive in a land where they were denied the fundamental rights, dignity, and respect that belong to all human beings. This is the story that we must tell."[20] A vote was scheduled for the following day, November 19, and the bill passed the House by an overwhelming margin, 409 to 9.

Victory was in sight. Nonetheless, even though Brownback had been able to get the bill passed once before, nothing was left to chance. He knew that the President supported this museum, and he had been communicating all along with White House officials behind the scenes. Thus, Brownback asked the White House to give the bill a boost.

Ron Christie, a member of the White House domestic policy staff, had been following the House bill. He saw it pass in the House, and he learned that Senator Brownback was seeking the President's support to help pass the bill in the Senate by unanimous consent and enact it into law as soon as possible. Christie brought the issue to Andrew Card, the President's Chief of Staff, and Card took Christie to the Oval Office to brief President Bush. Bush was pleased to learn of the House passage, and he picked up the phone and called Senator Bill Frist, Republican of Tennessee and the Majority Leader, to communicate his views.

The next day, when the enrolled House bill arrived at the Senate, Frist sought unanimous consent for its consideration by the full chamber. Then, Frist yielded the floor to Brownback. As Lewis had done two days earlier, Brownback thanked the bill's many essential supporters. And while he acknowledged that this museum would not be a panacea for healing race relations in America, he expressed his hope that "this museum will be a catalyst for needed racial reconciliation in this country. There will be many tears shed at this museum—tears that cleanse the soul and that transcend race, creed, and color."

Brownback also explained that this museum was necessary to help all Americans understand the development of our nation, noting that "[w]ith the creation of this museum, we will celebrate a rich and magnificent history. A history of a people's quest for freedom that shaped this Nation into a symbol of freedom and democracy around the world."[21]

Moments after Brownback resumed his seat, the bill passed the full Senate without objection. Once again, a compromise bill had moved with warp speed. Introduced in the House on November 17, it passed the Senate only three days later.

In one of the proudest moments of my life, I found myself in the White House waiting to enter the Oval Office to watch President Bush sign the bill into law. Once again, I would have the privilege of being a witness to history.

It was hard to believe that the official establishment of the National Museum of African American History and Culture was only moments away. I, and the other commissioners present, congratulated Wright and Brown, our leaders, for guiding us in such an able fashion. I shook hands with Secretary Small, satisfied that we were now there, together, on one accord. But the most gratifying sight was Lewis and Brownback, who were overtaken with emotion with the realization their unlikely partnership had produced, finally, this incredible result.

We were called into the Oval Office, and President Bush exuberantly greeted each one of us as we made our way inside, single file. Standing directly behind him, between Lewis and Brownback, I watched as the President put pen to paper. I thought of Ferdinand Lee, Mary Church Terrell, and so many others who had worked so hard for this museum, but who had not lived to see this day (figure 9).

Proud and elated as I was, I could not yet exhale. The decision by the Smithsonian Board of Regents on the museum's location still loomed.

Though our first choice of the Capitol site had been removed from the list, our second choice, the Monument site, was among the four options in the law, and it had been our second choice only by a hair. I believe most on the commission considered the two locations as basically equal in merit. As such, I felt like my job was not yet completed. I was determined to do

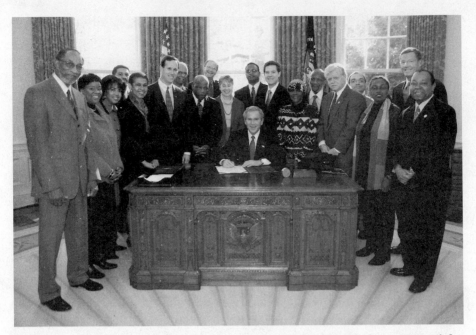

Figure 9. From left, pictured are: Dr. Robert Wright; Renee' Amoore; Vicky Bailey; Andrew McLemore, Jr.; Delegate Eleanor Holmes Norton, D-D.C.; Senator Rick Santorum, R-Penn.; Dr. Michael Lomax; Congressman John Lewis, D-Ga.; Dr. Harold Skramstad, Jr.; Barbara Franco; Robert Wilkins; Senator Sam Brownback, R-Kan.; Cicely Tyson; Lerone Bennett, Jr.; Congressman John Larson, D-Conn.; Dr. Eric Sexton; Claudine Brown; Larry Small, Secretary of the Smithsonian Institution; Currie Ballard. [22]

what I could to see the commission's wish fulfilled, to secure this site on the National Mall, adjacent to the Washington Monument. Dr. Wright, our chair, felt the same.

As a result, Dr. Wright and I continued to push the issue. I met with Roger Sant, chair of the executive committee of the Smithsonian Board of Regents, to brief him on the commission's actions and conclusions. I wanted to make sure he understood the history and the context, to be certain all of our efforts and deliberations did not go to waste. I knew the Smithsonian would hire its own consultants and study the issue yet again, but I needed to ensure the commission's position was fully understood. Sant was thoughtful and gracious, and the billionaire energy executive even invited me to a follow-up meeting at his Georgetown mansion.

The legislation authorizing the museum called for an Advisory Council, and when I learned that appointments to the council were being made, I discovered that one of the appointees was Frank Raines, previously head of Fannie Mae. One of the members of my nonprofit, Patrice Alexander Ficklin, knew Raines from her prior employment at Fannie Mae, and she arranged for us to meet with him. We briefed him on the commission's recommendations, what had transpired in Congress, and who was against our efforts, in hope that the Advisory Council would join the commission's position and use its influence with the Smithsonian Board of Regents to push for the Monument site.

Our meeting turned out to be just insurance. In a masterful move, the Regents appointed Dr. Michael Lomax, a member of the Presidential Commission, to the Advisory Council. Because of Lomax's appointment, and because the legislation specified that at least one member of the Board of Regents also serve on the Advisory Council, we were assured that the commission's institutional memory would be passed on to the Advisory Council, and then up the next level, to the Board of Regents.

But I could leave nothing to chance, because I knew that the NCPC, the National Park Service, and the Coalition, among others, were lobbying the Smithsonian Regents hard to choose the Banneker Overlook site and reject the Monument site.[23] Instead, the Presidential Commission had spoken clearly and unanimously, and we had firmly concluded, based on all of the evidence, that the Monument site was the best location for this museum.

So, my work was not done.

I battled back by providing letters and memoranda to Sant, Secretary Small, and the Advisory Council about the history of the museum effort, the plans for the Mall, the siting of other museums, the deliberations of the Presidential Commission, and the responses to the objections to the Monument site. I wanted everyone to have a clear understanding of the commission's views and the reasons behind them. By law, the Chief Justice of the United States serves as a Smithsonian Regent and by long tradition he is the Smithsonian's Chancellor. So I also briefed Sally Rider, the top assistant to then-Chief Justice William H. Rehnquist.

President Bush stepped in once again to provide a vital boost. On February 8, 2005, during a White House reception in honor of Black History Month, Bush announced his preference that the museum be located on the National Mall. In heartfelt remarks, Bush recounted his visit to Goree Island in Senegal with the First Lady, and how he stood in the 'Door of No Return' and felt "gut-wrenching" pain as he saw "the cramped cells where Africans were held right before they began their journey to America in chains." He continued by saying, "as I think back to standing in that door, it reminds me how important the museum is going to be, because young Americans study this shameful period in history in their schools, and they read their textbooks, but most young Americans will never go to Goree Island or get the same sense that we felt."

In front of Brownback, Cicely Tyson, members of the Advisory Council, and many other museum supporters, Bush concluded his remarks by declaring that he "want[ed] to make it clear to our fellow citizens, we have a chance to build a fantastic museum, right here in the heart of Washington, D.C., on the Mall, to stand proud."[24] What a special moment, particularly since a newly elected senator named Barack Obama was also in the audience.

Now, the matter lay in the hands of the Smithsonian Board of Regents, the august seventeen-member body made up of the Chief Justice, the Vice President, three Senators, three Representatives, and nine private citizens. On January 30, 2006, the Regents made their decision.

Immediately following the Regents' meeting, Sant, the chair of the Executive Committee, and Dr. Walter Massey, the Regent who also served on the museum's Advisory Council, announced the selection of the Monument site. They explained that, after considering all of the studies and input they had received, a wide majority of the Regents favored that location, particularly given the site's symbolism for this museum. They also noted that this was the first meeting attended by Chief Justice John G. Roberts, Jr., whom President Bush had appointed just a few months earlier to succeed Chief Justice Rehnquist upon his passing.

I did not know Chief Justice Roberts then, but he later told me that, when he met with White House lawyers after being nominated to the office, they mentioned that one of his additional duties, if confirmed, was to serve as Chancellor of the Smithsonian. Not to worry, they told him, because most matters that came before the Board of Regents were routine and uncontroversial. He laughed when recounting the guidance, given that, at his very first meeting, the Regents had to decide where to locate the National Museum of African American History and Culture, a matter that was far from mundane.

Lonnie G. Bunch III, the Smithsonian's exceptional hire as Founding Director of the Museum, also spoke, thanking the Regents for selecting what he believed was the best site, and telling them that he did not know if he would ever stop smiling following this monumental decision. Bunch also thanked Secretary Small and Undersecretary Burke, who were present. The three of them then answered logistical questions about the next steps and explained how the Smithsonian was going to support this museum so that it could open by 2016.

As I look back at that press conference, I have a much better appreciation for Small and Burke. Previously, I had been upset at what I believed to be their unjustified objections to the museum. I now understand that, as the top managers of the Smithsonian with the concomitant fiduciary responsibilities, they were working to protect the Institution, and they had had valid concerns given the unfunded capital needs of existing museums and the uneven political support for an African American museum in the past. Once Congress got fully on board, particularly key appropriators like Senator Ted Stevens, Republican of Alaska and the powerful chairman of the appropriations committee, and once the Regents gave their blessing, Small and Burke got squarely behind the museum and skillfully moved the project forward. Their duty now encompassed this museum, and they were devoted to fulfilling it.

When I learned of the Regents' decision, all I could do was exclaim, "Thank God!"

The unanimous vision of the Presidential Commission had been fulfilled, and I felt that I had finally accomplished the mission I began when I volunteered to chair the site and building committee years earlier. This was one of the most important tasks I had undertaken in my entire life, and I had carried it out as best I could. As a lawyer, it felt like my team and I just won the trial of the century, in which we had convinced a jury that included billionaires, Senators, and the Vice President, along with a foreman who happened to be the Chief Justice of the United States.

What a phenomenal journey.

EPILOGUE

★

OVER THE FINISH LINE

With the selection of the museum's site, my official role in this venture came to an end. When I first got involved with the project, my dream was to be a catalyst, to help get the ball rolling and pave the way for the experts with the vision, wisdom, and expertise to bring the museum to fruition. But when the time came to hand the baton to the Smithsonian, the gravity of the situation weighed on me. So much work remained to be done. The building needed to be designed and constructed, the artifacts collected, the exhibits conceived, and lots and lots of money raised. The list of needs seemed daunting.

Fortunately, with this project under the excellent leadership of Founding Director Lonnie Bunch, I knew the museum was in good hands. And by any measure, events since the official site selection have confirmed that assessment. Bunch put together a tremendous team, beginning with Deputy Director Kinshasha Holman Conwill. Together, Bunch and Conwill hired dozens of extremely talented curators, designers, and other professional and administrative staff. They also launched an international design competition for the museum building, which yielded a magnificent design by a brilliant team of architects, David Adjaye, Phillip Freelon, and the late Max Bond. Their building makes a bold and beautiful statement, with its crown-like shape formed by three tiers of ornamental corona panels, inspired by West African art, that wrap the structure and create a distinctive facade.

Indeed, the building itself makes history, as the first museum on the National Mall primarily designed by architects of African descent.

Despite early concerns, this iconic building will be far from empty. As of this writing, the museum staff had digitized more than one million images and amassed a collection of greater than 34,000 artifacts and works of art.[1] Bunch and the curatorial staff were greatly assisted in this effort by the guidance of the museum's Scholar Advisory Council. Preeminent historian John Hope Franklin served as Founding Chairman of this body until his passing in 2009, and its members provided valuable direction to Bunch and his staff as they undertook the difficult task of deciding what stories this museum should tell and how it should tell them.

No museum can be built without substantial financial resources, and this one has cost roughly $540 million to create. Congress delivered on the public share, as set forth in the legislation, to fund half, and with the leadership, generosity, and hard work of the museum's Advisory Council, Bunch already has raised more than $330 million in private funds.[2]

Remarkably, this sum of contributions is almost three times the amount that the Presidential Commission estimated in our study as an achievable private fundraising goal. The drive was led by Linda Johnson Rice and Richard Dean Parsons, co-chairs of the Advisory Council, with active engagement of all the other dedicated members of that body, including Oprah Winfrey. The Smithsonian has published several books and articles that ably describe the details of this and other essential and diligent work that went into bringing this museum over the finish line. Rather than duplicate those works, I commend them to you.[3]

Prior to stepping aside and letting the real experts take over back in 2002, I had returned to practicing law full-time, joining the firm of Venable LLP just after my appointment to the Presidential Commission. Shortly after I started there, I learned the partnership had made a real estate decision that truly stirred my soul.

Venable was moving into a newly renovated historic structure that had formerly been the Hecht's Department Store, a Washington institution. After sitting empty for well over a decade, it had been gut-renovated, converted to office space, and given a new moniker, *Terrell Place*. The name honored Mary Church Terrell, who had helped lead the campaign to desegregate the Hecht's lunch counter in the early 1950's. In a case that went all the way to the Supreme Court of the United States in 1953, Terrell and her compatriots prevailed over Jim Crow by use of a District of Columbia public accommodations law. The Supreme Court held that segregation was illegal in Washington, D.C., and that the lunch counter must be open to all. In the year before *Brown v. Board of Education* was decided, Terrell struck an important blow against institutionalized bigotry.[4]

To honor her legacy, the firm and the building owners installed a lobby display celebrating Terrell's contribution to American life. In addition to the exhibit, three stunning life-sized bronze sculptures portraying Terrell's life's work in pursuit of education, liberty, and equality were installed inside the building's entrance. These three beautiful and graceful depictions of strong Black women were commissioned from the famed African American artist, Elizabeth Catlett.[5] In another thrill, I had the opportunity to meet Ms. Catlett when she came to inspect the installation of her work as well as to assist the designers as they conceived the Mary Church Terrell exhibit.

As described in earlier chapters, Mary Church Terrell and her husband, Judge Robert H. Terrell, were involved with the National Memorial Association from its inception in 1916, and in 1929, Mary Church Terrell was appointed to serve on the presidential commission created to construct what was to be known as the National Memorial Building to Negro Achievement and Contributions to America. As I unpacked my boxes and settled into my new office, I was struck by the notion that here I was, trying to finish the work through our Commission that Mary Church Terrell had started with the 1929 commission, and I was working in a building where she had once been rejected, a building she had helped to rid of discrimination so that I could now, as an African American, eat in the office cafeteria without giving it a second thought.

The connection floored me, and it signaled to me that a greater power was guiding my involvement in this project. That belief helped sustain me on dark days while serving on the Presidential Commission when obstacles to the museum emerged to block our path, and it helped order my steps as I sought a way around those obstructions. I felt God's hand propping me up and pushing me along, so that the labor of Mary Church Terrell and so many others would not be in vain.

The beauty of the African American story is that the toil of our people has not been in vain. As President Obama has observed, exhibits in this museum that depict strife and loss simultaneously depict progress. "[W]hen future generations hear the songs of pain and progress and struggle and sacrifice, I hope they will not think of them as somehow separate from the larger American story. I want them to see it as central—an important part of our shared story. A call to see ourselves in one another. A call to remember that each of us is made in God's image. That's the history we will preserve within these walls. The history of a people who, in the words of Dr. King, 'injected new meaning and dignity into the veins of civilization.'"[6]

As the Smithsonian puts it, this museum will tell "a people's journey [and] a nation's story."

But if the African American journey is indeed the nation's story, why did it take one-hundred years to create this museum? James Baldwin gave us the answer when, as described earlier, he told a Congressional committee in 1968, "My history contains the truth about America. It is going to be hard to teach it." Indeed, Lonnie Bunch has made clear that the utmost priority of this museum will be, in John Hope Franklin's words, always to "tell the unvarnished truth."[7] But telling the hard truth is not always easy, nor is it always popular.

Telling this hard truth in the nation's capital was a difficult concept for the National Memorial Association to get Congress to accept in the 1920s. As I have recounted, southern members of Congress stated openly on the floors of the House and Senate that Black people were lucky to have been brought to America and saved from their "uncivilized" existence in Africa. They mocked the idea that African Americans had made any real achievements or contributions to America. Indeed, they favored a monument to the Black Mammy over one to the Black soldier.

These views helped justify the two-tiered system of American citizenship they favored. If African Americans were indeed inferior in intellect, character, and resolve, then twisted logic could justify relegating them to second-class citizenship. Celebrating African American achievement was inconsistent with subjugation.

Similar racist attitudes even infected genteel institutions such as the Smithsonian. As Smithsonian Undersecretary Dr. Richard Kurin has recounted, in the 1940s, museum officials initially refused to accept the donation of the Medal of Honor bestowed upon Christian Fleetwood, a Black Union soldier, for his heroism during the Civil War. The gift from Fleetwood's descendants would have been rebuffed but for the personal intervention of the Secretary of the Smithsonian.[8] Just as the achievement of the Black Union soldier was excluded from celebration during the Grand Review, the achievement of the Black Union soldier was for too long excluded from celebration in America's national museum.

Our country has also avoided the hard truth because, quite simply, the hard truth hurts. Bunch warns us that, "this will be a Museum that will have moments to make one cry, [and] ponder the pain of slavery and segregation." Let's face it: an honest look at the history of America's treatment of

African Americans takes us to a very dark place. It is a place where Blacks were bought and sold like chattel, exploited for centuries without compensation, beaten and raped without compunction, and lynched for sport. It is a place where humanity, compassion, and decency were often sorely absent.

I cannot imagine how exhibits that bear true witness to the degradation and evil of the institutions of slavery and Jim Crow could avoid inflicting pain, or shame, on the observer. These are not the happy stories we like to see and hear, the stories to which we escape for pleasure and entertainment. When viewed in that context, congressional reluctance to help create a museum that would tell these painful stories is understandable. Yet these stories must be told.

Hard truth is also painful because it fosters self-examination, forcing us to consider profound questions about the meaning of America and our institutions. On the one hand, we look across the National Mall and see monuments to Washington, the father of our country, and Jefferson, the author of our Declaration of Independence. These men made heroic efforts to form the nation and establish the foundations of our government. But this museum will tell the story of the ugly, evil institution of slavery that they participated in, benefited from, and sanctioned at the same time. How do we explain to ourselves and our children why these men are worthy of prominent monuments on the Mall, while standing inside a museum and viewing exhibits that display the evil that these men tolerated and endorsed?

Former First Lady Laura Bush, who serves on the museum's Advisory Council, has supplied a compelling answer. At the museum groundbreaking, she noted that it was only fitting that this museum would rise adjacent to the monument to our first president, a slave owner. That is because, "side-by-side, these two spots are symbolic of our own national journey. For the stories that will be preserved within these walls, the stories of suffering and perseverance, of daring, of imagination, and of triumph are the stories of African Americans. But they are also stories that are forever woven through the heart of the fabric of our nation."[9] The good deeds of Washington and Jefferson are integral to the American story, but so are the bad deeds. One does not erase the other. Together, they tell the unvarnished truth of our nation's journey.

The bipartisan coalition that authorized this museum wisely saw that America was mature enough to handle the hard truth, to understand that, even if our union is not perfect, we have a continuing obligation, in the words of the preamble of the Constitution, to make it "more perfect."[10] This bipartisan coalition had the courage to face the hard truth of African

American history because they knew that, even though it would cause some pain, and perhaps some shame, a fulsome examination of this history will help us learn from the past and think about how we can come together as a nation.

Even the physical design of the museum reflects the path of hard truth. As is fitting, the main history galleries are located below the earth. Visitors must descend five stories below grade, into the bowels of the building, to view the exhibits on slavery. As they work their way through history, the visitor path leads up toward the surface. By the time they finish examining the Civil Rights Movement of the 1960s, visitors are just below grade, where they come to an area called the "contemplative court," a place to sit and reflect on the power of the story. While resting, visitors will gaze at a circular glass tube with water cascading down its outer edges, and if they look through the water and up into the tube, through a window called an oculus, they can glimpse the sky.[11] After coming out of the darkness, they will be able to see the light.

At that point, symbolically speaking, it is time to come up for air. The galleries above ground house collections of music and art, sports and culture. These exhibits also cover aspects of history, of course, but they will primarily explore brighter themes after the deep, dark dive into the past.

I imagine that many visitors will pause a good long time between the darkness and the light, sitting at the contemplative court, reflecting on the hard truths they have seen and experienced. It is my hope that, through this reflection, the museum will fulfill its true mission: to bring healing and understanding to a country in need. Like a long-overdue intervention, perhaps it will clear the air and make way for new understandings and better relationships within the American family.

I am certain that I will need the respite of the contemplative court, as I know emotional exhaustion will overcome me after each journey through the history galleries. I have no doubt that I will feel great pain and anger as I reflect on the first part of the museum. And as I reflect, I will be compelled to ponder my own story.

It is the story of a son raised by his single mother, a story in which, despite having meager family resources, I had the opportunity to attend excellent, integrated public schools. A story in which I was able to go on to Rose-Hulman Institute of Technology, one of the top engineering colleges in the nation, and then on to Harvard Law School, another leading institution. Although I have felt the sting of discrimination in my lifetime, America has blessed me with great opportunity, and made the path for me easier than that laid before my parents, my grandparents, and the generations preceding them. Viewing the past will be painful, but the knowledge of our progress will be a salve.

There is no denying American's evolution. Nor can we deny that the path has been improbable. How does one explain a journey that on one end has President Hoover refusing to allow Addison Scurlock to take his photograph with Mary Church Terrell and the other members of the commission formed to create this museum, but eighty years later, features, as the very first exhibit created by the National Museum of African of African American History and Culture, an exhibition of Scurlock's photos of prominent African Americans?[12]

How does one explain a road that begins with denial and rejection against the backdrop of the racist screed that is *Birth of a Nation*, but that ends, four generations later, with the museum opening with the support of an African American president and luminaries like Oprah Winfrey and Cicely Tyson, who promote positive images of African Americans on film? How do I explain a path in which I befriended that President, almost thirty years ago while we were both in law school, and that now will allow me to watch him throw open the doors to a museum into which I poured my heart and soul for so many years?

On that day, I will think about Mary Church Terrell. Recently, I learned that the wonderful sculptures in her honor were relocated from Terrell Place to a fitting new home. In a superb gesture, they were donated to the museum, where they will be part of the opening exhibition. Mary Church Terrell was once excluded from the picture; but now, she and her contributions to our great nation will be part of the story.

And that was the whole point.

NOTES

Prologue

1. "1995 Pulitzer Prizes, Journalism," The Pulitzer Prizes—Columbia University, accessed August 5, 2016, http://www.pulitzer.org/prize-winners-by-year/1995.

Chapter 1

1. *Army and Navy Journal*, May 13, 1865, 601.
2. "News from Washington," *New York Times*, May 6, 1865, 4.
3. David W. Blight, *Race and Reunion: The Civil War in American Memory* (Cambridge, Mass.: Belknap, 2001), 64.
4. "The Grand Review," *Frank Leslie's Weekly*, June 10, 1865.
5. *New York Tribune*, May 24, 1865, 1.
6. *New York Sun*, May 24, 1865, 1.
7. "The Grand Review in Washington," *Daily Intelligencer*, May 25, 1865, 3.
8. Edmund N. Hatcher, *The Last Four Weeks of the War* (Columbus: Edmund N. Hatcher, 1891), 382.
9. "General Butler on Confiscation," *The Liberator*, June 23, 1865.
10. "Emancipation League," *The Liberator*, June 2, 1865, 87.
11. *National Anti-Slavery Standard*, June 3, 1865, 1.
12. Samuel P. Bates, *History of Pennsylvania Volunteers, 1861–5, Vol V.*, (Harrisburg: B. Singerly, 1871), 1011; Frederick H. Dyer, *A Compendium of the War of the Rebellion, Compiled and Arranged From Official Records of the Federal and Confederate Armies, Reports of the Adjutant Generals of the Several States, the Army Registers, and Other Reliable Documents and Sources* (Des Moines: Dyer Publishing Co., 1908), 1727.
13. Caroline E. Janney, *Remembering the Civil War: Reunion and the Limits of Reconciliation* (Chapel Hill: University of North Caroline Press, 2013), 71 (quoting *The Liberator*, June 2, 1865).
14. "Colored Solders! Welcome! Welcome!" *The Christian Recorder*, Oct. 28, 1865, 171.
15. Ibid.
16. "Universal Suffrage," *The Christian Recorder*, June 24, 1865.
17. "Should the Negro Enlist in the Union Army?" Address at a Meeting for the Promotion of Colored Enlistments, July 6, 1863, published in *Douglass' Monthly*, Aug. 1863.

18. *New York Times*, May 23, 1865, accessed August 5, 2016, http://www.nytimes.com/1865/05/23/news/southwest-reported-assassination-rebel-general-kirby-smith-capture-ex-gov-isham.html.

19. Bobby L. Lovett, "The Negro's Civil War in Tennessee, 1861–1865," *Journal of Negro History* 61, no. 1 (1976): 43–45.

20. H.R. Rep. No. 38–65, at 4 (1864).

21. *New York Times*, May 26, 1865, accessed August 5, 2016, http://www.nytimes.com/1865/05/26/news/southwest-denial-story-kirby-smith-s-assassination-his-wife-says-some-his-men.html.

22. "The Habit of Prejudice, and Denial of Right," *National Anti-Slavery Standard*, July 1, 1865; *Frank Leslie's Weekly*, June 10, 1865; *National Anti-Slavery Standard*, June 3, 1865.

23. C. R. Gibbs, *Black, Copper and Bright: The District of Columbia's Black Civil War Regiment* (Silver Spring, Md.: Three Dimensional Pub., 2002), 57.

24. John Savage, *The Life and Public Services of Andrew Johnson, Seventeenth President of the United States, Including His State Papers, Speeches and Addresses* (New York: Derby & Miller, 1866), Speech to the Negro Soldiers, Oct. 10, 1865 appears at Appendix 90–95. All quotes from President Johnson's speech come from this source.

25. "The Review," *Washington Evening Star*, May 22, 1865, 2.

26. *Daily National Republican*, second edition, Oct. 11, 1865, 2, http://chronicling-america.loc.gov/lccn/sn86053570/1865-10-11/ed-1/seq-2/.

27. "The President's Speech," *National Anti-Slavery Standard*, Oct. 21, 1865.

28. Ibid.

29. George W. Williams, *A History of the Negro Troops in The War of the Rebellion 1861–1865* (New York: Harper & Brothers, 1888), 328.

30. Ibid.

31. "Reunion of colored veterans," *New York Times*, Aug. 3, 1887, 5.

32. John Hope Franklin, *George Washington Williams: A Biography* (Durham, N.C.: Duke University Press, 1998), 171–74.

33. Captain James M. Wells, *With Touch of Elbow or Death Before Dishonor: A Thrilling Narrative of Adventure on Land and Sea* (Philadelphia: John C. Winston Co., 1909), 271.

34. As we will see, many who would come after Williams worked to ensure a satisfactory answer to that question. Fittingly, John Hope Franklin became one of many who helped bring Williams's quest for legacy to fruition, serving as the first Chair of the Scholarly Advisory Committee of the National Museum of African American History and Culture until his passing in 2009. Prior to the realization of the national museum dedicated to the entirety of African American history, Frank Smith, a former member of the D.C. City Council, helped lead the effort to build the African American Civil War Memorial and Museum in the Shaw neighborhood of Washington, not far from Howard University.

Chapter 2

1. Wallace E. Davies, "The Problem of Race Segregation in the Grand Army of the Republic," *Journal of Southern History* 13, no. 1 (1947): 356–57.
2. John Hope Franklin, "*Birth of a Nation*—Propaganda as History," *Massachusetts Review* 20, no. 3 (1979): 417–34.
3. Robert Lang, *The Birth of a Nation: D.W. Griffith, Director* (New Brunswick, NJ: Rutgers University Press, 1994), 43–156. These initial pages generally provide a continuity script of the film, describing the entirety of the film in detail, shot by shot. Pages especially of note are 103–04, 107–08.
4. Ibid.
5. Ibid. at 114–15, 134.
6. Ibid. at 155.
7. Rev. A. J. Emerson, "The Birth of a Nation," *Confederate Veteran* 24, no. 3 (1916): 141.
8. "Facts about 'The Birth of a Nation,'" *Washington Herald*, Apr. 11, 1915, 19.
9. Ibid.
10. See article by John Hope Franklin.
11. August Meier and John H. Bracey, Jr., "The NAACP as a Reform Movement, 1909–1965: 'To Reach the Conscience of America,'" *Journal of Southern History* 59, no. 1 (1993): 3–30.
12. Melvyn Stokes, *D.W. Griffith's The Birth of a Nation: A History of the Most Controversial Motion Picture of All Time* (Oxford: Oxford University Press, 2007): 129–70
13. Ibid. at 424–25.
14. "White House Will Have Movie Show," *Washington Times*, Feb. 18, 1915, 1; "President to See Movies," *Evening Star* (Washington, D.C.), Feb. 18, 1915, 1. It was widely rumored and reported that after seeing the film, President Wilson exclaimed, "it is like writing history with lightning. And my only regret is that it is also terribly true." See Mark E. Benbow, "Birth of a Quotation: Woodrow Wilson and 'Like Writing History with Lightning,'" *Journal of the Gilded Age and Progressive Era* 9, no. 4 (2010): 509–33. Whether Wilson ever made such a statement is the subject of much debate, but the rumor no doubt gave credence to the belief that granting equal rights to Black people would harm the nation.
15. "Chief Justice and Senators at Movie," *Washington Herald*, Feb. 20, 1915, 4; "Movies at Press Club," *Washington Post*, Feb. 20, 1915, 5; "The Birth of a Nation," *The Sun* (New York), Feb. 22, 1915, 7.
16. "Birth of a Nation Brings Wilson Worry," *Washington Herald*, May 1, 1915, 6; "Dixon's Play Is Not Indorsed By Wilson," *Washington Times*, Apr. 30, 1915, 6; Benbow, "Birth of a Quotation," 509–33.
17. "Special Services to be Held in Washington Churches Tomorrow in Recognition of G.A.R. Encampment," *Evening Star*, Sept. 25, 1915, 10; "Birth of a Nation to Be Told to GAR," *The Washington Times*, Sept. 25, 1915, 11.
18. *Washington Bee*, Sept. 25, 1915.
19. *Evening Star*, Sept. 24, 1915, 2.
20. *Washington Herald*, Sept. 26, 1915, 10.

21. Letter dated Sept. 10, 1915, from President Wilson's papers in the Library of Congress.
22. *Journal of the 49th National Encampment of the Grand Army of the Republic*, H. Doc. 64-469, 209–11 (1916). All quotes from President Wilson's speech to the Encampment come from this source.
23. Id. at 252; "Veterans Parade through Capitol of Nation They Save," *Evening Star*, Sept. 29, 1915, 1; "President Waives Cordial Greeting to Old Soldiers," *Evening Star*, Sept. 29, 1915, 1.
24. *Journal of the 49th National Encampment*, 248; "Wilson weeps as withered GAR veterans repeat review of '65," *New York Tribune*, Sept. 30, 1915; "Ex-Confederates March in Parade," *Washington Times*, Sept. 29, 1915, 1.
25. "Fifty Years," *Afro-American Ledger*, Oct. 2, 1915, 4.
26. "Colored Citizens Planning Entertainment for Members of Their Race," *Evening Star*, Sept. 5, 1915, 3.
27. Letter from National Memorial Association, Inc. to President Woodrow Wilson, July 20, 1916, Woodrow Wilson Papers, Library of Congress.
28. "Fifty Years," *Afro-American Ledger*, Oct. 2, 1915, 4.

Chapter 3

1. S. Doc. 63-621, 33–34 (1914).
2. "DAR History," Daughters of the American Revolution, accessed August 5, 2016, http://www.dar.org/national-society/about-dar/dar-history.
3. "Letter to F. D. Lee," Records of the Board of Commissioners for the District of Columbia, National Archives 97 (1916): 221406; "Memo appointing Commissioner Brownlow to confer with National Memorial Association," Records of the Board of Commissioners for the District of Columbia, National Archives 97 (1916): 221404. The Commission of Fine Arts was a planning body created by Congress in 1910 to oversee the design and aesthetics of Washington, D.C.'s architecture.
4. Members of the NMA's executive board had helped lead the petition drive to ban *The Birth of a Nation*, and two of the speakers for the planning meeting—Isabella Worrell Ball and Reverend W.H. Jernagin—had endorsed earlier resolutions urging the commissioners to ban the film.
5. "Would bar Negroes from Army or Navy," *Daily Arkansas Gazette*, July 29, 1916, 12.
6. 53 Cong. Rec. 12,688–89 (1916) (statement of Rep. Caraway).
7. Ibid., 12689.
8. "Read The Following Bills," *Crisis* 13, no. 1 (November 1916): 39–40, http://library.brown.edu/pdfs/1292419668523500.pdf.
9. 53 Cong. Rec. 2,224 (1916).
10. "Start a Memorial," *Washington Bee*, December 20, 1919.
11. "Asks for no marble shaft," *Baltimore Afro-American*, December 19, 1919; "Colonel Charles Young at Saint Mark's Church," *New York Age*, December 20, 1919.
12. Barbara Holden-Smith, "Lynching, Federalism, and the Intersection of Race and Gender in the Progressive Era," *Yale Journal of Law and Feminism* 31 (1996): 8.

13. 57 Cong. Rec. 176 (1919) (statement of Rep. Kahn).

14. John R. Hawkins, an NMA founder, and Reverend William H. Jernagin sent an official petition to Congress on behalf of the National Race Congress, asking for federal legislation to prohibit lynching and eliminate racial discrimination in accommodations, interstate travel, elections, labor relations, and in the court system. 58 Cong. Rec. 7046 (1919). This petition sought many of the redresses ultimately granted by the Civil Rights Acts of the 1960s.

15. 58 Cong. Rec. 6,639-40 (1919) (statement of Rep. Heflin).

16. 57 Cong. Rec. 4,644-45 (1919) (statement of Rep. Dyer).

17. 65 Cong. Rec. 10,540 (1924) (statement of Rep. Dyer).

18. H. Rep. 70-853, 2 (1928).

19. A Bill Authorizing the Erection in the City of Washington of a Monument in Memory of the Faithful Colored Mammies of the South, S. 4119, 67th Cong. (1922); ibid., H.R. 13672, 67th Cong (1923); ibid., H.R. 6253, 68th Cong. (1924).

20. "Charlotte Hawkins Brown Speaks at Oberlin College," *New York Age*, February 3, 1923; "Futile Monument Scheme," *New York Age*, March 3, 1923; "The Southern Paradox," *New York Age*, March 24, 1923.

21. 65 Cong. Rec. 4,839 (1923).

22. When the bill to create a national memorial building for African Americans was finally passed in 1929, the designer of a "mammy o' mine" memorial statue inspired by the colored mammy memorial legislation had the gall to request the placement of her statue in the memorial building. *Letter from Ethel L. Carpenter to the Commission on Fine Arts* dated Oct. 25, 1929, Files of the Commission on Fine Arts, National Archives.

23. Hearings on H.J. Res. 60, Before the Comm. on Public Buildings & Grounds, 70th Cong. 5 (1928) (hereafter 1928 Hearings).

24. Walker was not only the first African American woman to become a self-made millionaire, she was also the first American woman of any race to do so. Walker made her fortune providing hair care products for Black women. Madam C.J. Walker, accessed August 5, 2016, http://www.madamcjwalker.com/#&panel1-1.

25. 1928 Hearings, 6.

26. Ibid., 7.

27. Ibid., 8.

28. Ibid., 14–15.

29. Ibid., 16–17.

30. Ibid., 18.

31. Mary Church Terrell was also the widow of Judge Robert Terrell, one of the founders of the NMA.

32. 1928 Hearings, 22 (statement of Mrs. Mary Church Terrell, First President of National Association of Colored Women).

33. 69 Cong. Rec. 10,592 (1928).

34. 70 Cong. Rec. 5,080 (1929) (statement of Rep. Taylor).

35. Ibid.

36. Ibid. The Jefferson Memorial was constructed and opened in 1943.

37. President Herbert Hoover was inaugurated later that day.

Chapter 4

1. J.H. Howard, "Memorial to Race Soldiers 'An Empty Honor,'" *Pittsburgh Courier*, March 30, 1929, 2.

2. Letter from Mordecai W. Johnson to Walter H. Newton (Secretary to President Hoover), August 10, 1929, Herbert Hoover Presidential Library; Letter of Nannie H. Burroughs to Walter H. Newton, August 14, 1929, Herbert Hoover Presidential Library; Letter of Nannie H. Burroughs to Walter H. Newton, September 4, 1929, Herbert Hoover Presidential Library.

3. "National Memorial Association Head Visiting in State," *New Journal and Guide*, September 14, 1929, 10.

4. Letter of National Memorial Association by Ferdinand Lee to Charles Moore, April 13, 1929, National Archives.

5. Letter from Samuel C. Smith (Executive Secretary of the National Memorial Association) to Charles Moore of April 25, 1929, Commission on Fine Arts files, National Archives.

6. Hawkins was also president of Prudential Bank in Washington, D.C.; the financial secretary of the National AME Church, and president of the Association for the Study of Negro Life and History.

7. Bethune was president and founder of both Bethune-Cookman College and the National Council of Negro Women. "Mary McLeod Bethune," National Council of Negro Women, accessed August 5, 2016, https://ncnw.org/about/bethune.htm.

8. Reverend Williams was the pastor of Mount Olivet Baptist Church in Chicago and president of the powerful National Baptist Convention. See "Lacey Kirk Williams," Texas State Historical Association, accessed August 5, 2016, https://tshaonline.org/handbook/online/articles/fwiag.

9. Pearson was a banker and insurance executive who founded the North Carolina Mutual and Provident Society, the precursor to North Carolina Mutual Life Insurance Company. See "William Gaston Pearson (Incorporator)," North Carolina Central University Digital Collection, accessed August 5, 2016, http://contentdm.auctr.edu/cdm/ref/collection/nccu/id/67.

10. Porter was a protégé of Booker T. Washington who became an attorney and the publisher of the *East Tennessee News* in Knoxville, Tennessee. He was also active in the National Negro Business League. Bobby L. Lovett, *The Civil Rights Movement in Tennessee: A Narrative History* (Knoxville, Univ. of Tenn. Press, 2005), 235.

11. Ransom, from Topeka, Kansas, was a Presiding Elder in the African Methodist Episcopal Church. "A.M.E. Boards Meet to Review Year's Work," New York Age, May 2, 1925, 2.

12. From Louisville, Kentucky, Weeden was the general secretary of the AME Zion Church and the author of *Weeden's History of the Colored People of Louisville*. "Henry Clay Weeden," Notable Kentucky African Americans Database, accessed August 5, 2016, http://nkaa.uky.edu/record.php?note_id=725.

13. Hueston was a state court judge from Gary, Indiana and a national officer of the International Brotherhood of the Elks.

14. From Los Angeles, California, Williams was the first African American fellow of the American Institute of Architects and later designed the Theme Building at Los Angeles International Airport (LAX). "Paul R. Williams, Architect," Paul R. Williams Project, accessed August 5, 2016, http://www.paulrwilliamsproject.org/about/paul-revere-williams-architect/.

15. Whittico was a city council member and the editor and publisher of the *Mc-Dowell Times* from Keystone, West Virginia. "Matthew T. Whittico," West Virginia Division of History & Culture, accessed August 5, 2016, http://www.wvculture.org/history/histamne/whitticm.html.

16. Jonathan P. Guy, et al., *Funding Study for the National Museum of African-American History and Culture*, December 3, 2002, 2–3 (on file with the author). After years of efforts by the Freedman's Bureau and the Secretaries of War to locate these Black veterans and their descendants, $325,553.21 in unpaid salaries and bounties were deposited into the United States Treasury.

17. Ibid., 3–8.

18. "Hoover photos are as scarce as his race appointments," *Baltimore Afro-American*, January 18, 1930, 1. Kenneth T. Walsh, *Family of Freedom: Presidents and African Americans in the White House* (Boulder: Paradigm, 2011), 81.

19. Ibid.

20. "Hoover poses again," *Baltimore Afro-American*, February 15, 1930, 3; "President hurt by flood of criticism," *Baltimore Afro-American*, November 22, 1930, 3; "Hoover talks Haiti with Commissioners," *Baltimore Afro-American*, October 25, 1930, 1.

21. "The Hoover Photographs, I told you so!" *Baltimore Afro-American*, October 8, 1932, 1.

22. "Leaders Talk with Hoover on Memorial," *Chicago Defender*, December 14, 1929, A1.

23. "Memorial Approved," *New York Telegram*, May 31, 1929. Although a prior study by the Commission on Fine Arts staff in 1920 had suggested the National Mall as the appropriate site for the memorial building, and some press reports during that period had stated similarly, there is no indication that the Commission on Fine Arts ever offered to help procure a Mall site for this project.

24. Hearings on H.J. Res. 60, Before the Comm. on Public Buildings & Grounds, 70th Cong. 23–26 (1928); Minutes of Meeting of the Commission on Fine Arts, April 25, 1929.

25. The proposed site was on Georgia Avenue directly across from the Howard University campus.

26. Letter of Ferdinand Lee to Charles Moore, December 12, 1929, National Archives.

27. Letter from Chairman Moore to Ferdinand Lee, January 9, 1930, Commission on Fine Arts files, National Archives.

28. Letter of David Lynn to Ferdinand Lee, December 30, 1929, Papers of the Architect of the Capitol.

29. Letter from A.W. Mellon to Walter H. Newton (Secretary to President Hoover) of February 25, 1930 (with attached report); Letter from Treasury

Undersecretary Ogden L. Mills to Walter H. Newton of May 19, 1930 (with attached reports), Hoover Presidential Library.

30. Joint Resolution to Amend Section 5 of the Joint Resolution Relating to the National Memorial Commission, S.J. Res. 171, 71st Cong. (1930). Letter from F.D. Lee to Senator Robert B. Howell, June 2, 1930, Herbert Hoover Presidential Library; Letter from F.D. Lee to Walter H. Newton (Secretary to President Hoover), June 16, 1930, Herbert Hoover Presidential Library.

31. Joint Resolution to Amend Section 5 of the Joint Resolution Relating to the National Memorial Commission, S.J. Res. 6, 72nd Cong. (1931).

32. "Fisk Jubilee Singers Win Acclaim in Concert Here," *Washington Post*, April 16, 1932, 12.

33. Letter from Ferdinand D. Lee to David Lynn (Architect of the Capitol), January 9, 1931, Papers of the Architect of the Capitol; "Paul Robeson in Recital," *Baltimore Afro American*, Jan. 24, 1931, 2; "6,000 Hear Robeson in Washington," *Philadelphia Tribune*, January 29, 1931, 6.

34. "Few Seats for Negros," *New York Herald Tribune*, March 30, 1931, 16; "DC Notables Hear Dett and Hampton Choir," *Baltimore Afro-American*, March 28, 1931, 3. Walter White, the National Secretary of the NAACP, protested the prejudice at the concert.

35. On March 7, 1933 Congressman Will Wood of Indiana, one of the most ardent champions of the Commission on Capitol Hill, passed away.

36. On April 1, 1933, Lee succumbed to illness at his home in Washington. He was buried in Harmony Cemetery just outside of Washington without even a marker.

37. Exec. Order No. 6166 § 2 (June 10, 1933).

38. "Expect National Negro Memorial Commission to be Abolished," *Baltimore Afro-American*, June 17, 1933, 18.

39. Letter from Samuel C. Smith (Executive Secretary of the National Memorial Association) to President Roosevelt of May 7, 1934, Franklin D. Roosevelt Presidential Library; Letter from M.H. McIntyre (Assistant Secretary to the President) to Samuel C. Smith, undated, Franklin D. Roosevelt Presidential Library.

40. Letter from Samuel C. Smith to President Roosevelt on May 6, 1935, Franklin D. Roosevelt Presidential Library; Letter from Marvin H. McIntyre to Samuel C. Smith of May 21, 1935, Franklin D. Roosevelt Presidential Library.

41. Joint Resolution Authorizing the Creation of a Federal Memorial Commission ... to the Memory of Thomas Jefferson, H.J. Res. 371, 73rd Cong. (1934).

Chapter 5

1. A Bill to Provide for the Establishment of the Negro History Commission, H.R. 10638, 89th Cong. (1965).

2. Hearing on H.R. 12962, *Before the Select Subcomm. on Labor of the H. Comm. on Education and Labor*, 90th Cong. 79 (1968) (hereinafter "1968 House Hearing") (statement of Charles H. Wright describing Rep. Powell's opposition to Rep. Scheuer's 1965 bill).

3.   A Bill to Provide for the Establishment of a Commission on Negro History and Culture, H.R. 12758, 90th Cong. (1967).

4.   H.R. Rep. No. 95-1828, pt. 2, at 277 (1979), http://www. archives.gov/research/jfk/select-committee-report/part-2-king-findings.html.

5.   1968 House Hearing, 39.

6.   Ibid., 37

7.   Ibid., 23.

8.   Ibid., 37.

9.   This museum is now called The Charles H. Wright Museum of African American History.

10. Mabel O. Wilson, *Negro Building* (Berkeley: University of California Press, 2012), 247.

11. Ibid., 283; Andrea A. Burns, *From Storefront to Monument: Tracing the Public History of the Black Museum Movement* (Amherst: University of Massachusetts Press, 2013), 160–64.

12. 1968 House Hearing, 57.

13. Ibid., 76.

14. Ibid., 78.

15. Ibid., 6.

16. Ibid., 56.

17. Ibid., 2.

18. Ibid., 62.

19. South Africa practiced apartheid, nationally sanctioned racial segregation in which White South Africans held all of the power and Black South Africans had little to none.

20. 1968 House Hearing, 64.

21. Ibid.

22. Baldwin's searing essays, plays, and novels frequently delved into the complicated and painful topic of race relations in America. On May 17, 1963, *Time* magazine featured Baldwin on the cover of an issue dedicated to "The Negro's Push for Equality." He was not initially expected to appear at this congressional committee hearing, and Congressman Scheuer expressed delight and surprise when Baldwin arrived. Betty Shabazz, the widow of Malcolm X, who had championed the study and promotion of Black history and culture, accompanied him.

23. 1968 House Hearing, 43.

24. Ibid., 42.

25. Ibid., 44.

26. Cassius Clay, who changed his name to Muhammad Ali in 1964, had been convicted of draft evasion for refusing to enter the Vietnam Conflict due to his Muslim faith and refusal to be a proponent of White supremacy. Martin Waldron, "Clay Guilty in Draft Case; Gets Five Years in Prison," *New York Times*, June 21, 1967, 1.

27. 1968 House Hearing, 42.

28. *Negro Building*, 289.

29. The conference highlighted the fact that many of the repositories containing important documents related to Black history were underfunded, underappreciated, and underutilized; and there was substantial concern that documents, letters, diaries, and other ephemera related to Black life and culture were either discarded or deteriorating in attics and basements around the country. Conference panelists also decried distorted and inaccurate historical accounts being taught in schools.

30. Hearing on S. 2979, *Before the Senate Special Subomm. on Arts & Humanities of the Comm. on Labor & Public Welfare*, 90th Cong. 10 (1968) (hereinafter "1968 Senate Hearing").

31. Ibid., 10.

32. Ibid., 11.

33. Ibid., 76.

34. The Black Power Movement of the 1960s and 1970s, a much more radical push for Black pride and autonomy than the broader civil rights movement, was direct about its quest for justice and anti-White supremacy stances.

35. 1968 Senate Hearing, 79–80.

36. Ibid., 80–81.

37. One of the first repositories for Black history and culture founded by Arturo Alfonso Schomburg, an Afro-Puerto Rican man, in response to his teacher's claim that Black people contributed nothing of value to history.

38. This is notable because various other agencies, including the Department of Agriculture, the Federal Communications Commission, the National Science Foundation, and the National Endowment of the Humanities, as well as the military, provided responses. In fact, Dr. Charles Wright had complained during the March 1968 House hearing that the Smithsonian, "has been more concerned with reptiles and birds than with Black Americans." 1968 House Hearing, 79.

39. These Councils led local efforts to maintain racial segregation in schools and public accommodations, as well as efforts to block Black people from voting.

40. 114 Cong. Rec. 27,017 (1968) (statement of Rep. Waggonner).

41. 113 Cong. Rec. 22,731 (1967) (statement of Rep. Selden).

42. In 1969, another bill was introduced, this time specifying that the commission would be known as the Commission on *Afro-American* History and Culture. Despite its new name, this bill also failed to pass.

43. 1968 House Hearing, 104 (statement of Rep. Brown entered into the open record following Dr. King's assassination on April 4, 1968).

44. Hearing on S.3419, *Before the Subcommittee on Parks and Recreation of the S. Committee on Interior and Insular Affairs*, 94th Cong. 40 (1976) (hereinafter "1976 Senate Hearing").

45. Glenn was the first American to orbit the Earth.

46. Senator Robert Taft Jr. of Ohio also supported the plan, as did Congressman Lewis Stokes, the first African American congressman from Ohio, and several other members of the Congressional Black Caucus: Congressmen Ron Dellums and Gus Hawkins from California, Congressmen John Conyers and

Charles Diggs from Michigan, Congressman Robert Nix from Pennsylvania, and Congressman Parren Mitchell from Maryland.

47. 1976 Senate Hearing, 45.
48. Among those appointed to the planning council were Senator Edward Brooke, Republican of Massachusetts, the first African American to join the U.S. Senate in eighty-five years; and Charles Wesley, the Executive Director of the Association for the Study of Afro-American Life and History.
49. 1976 Senate Hearing, 59.
50. Ibid., 12–13.
51. Pub. L. No. 94-518, Title III, § 301, 90 Stat. 2447 (1980).
52. Hearing on S. 1814, *Before the Senate Committee on Governmental Affairs*, 96th Cong. 9–11 (1980).
53. Ibid., 20, 27.
54. Pub. L. No. 96-430, Title II, 94 Stat. 1846 (1980) (codified at 20 U.S.C. § 3701).
55. There has been no indication the Commission ever completed its report.
56. Pub. L. No. 101-184, 103 Stat. 1336 (1989).

Chapter 6

1. Bill to Establish an American Slavery Memorial Council, H.R. 3829, 99th Cong. (1985).
2. Pub. L. No. 99-511, 100 Stat. 2080 (1986).
3. Kara Swisher, "Fanfare for a Museum," Washington Post, April 11, 1988, B1.
4. National African-American Heritage Museum and Memorial Act, H.R. 5305, 100th Cong. (1988).
5. Pub. L. No. 94-74, 89 Stat. 407 (1975); President Signs Legislation Reserving Mall Site for SI," *Smithsonian Torch*, September 1975, http://siarchives.si.edu/sites/default/files/pdfs/torch/1975/SIA_000371_1975_09.pdf.
6. Douglas E. Evelyn, "A Most Beautiful Sight Presented itself to My View: The Long Return to a Native Place on the Mall," in *Spirit of a Native Place: Building the National Museum of the American Indian*, ed. Duane Blue Spruce (Washington, D.C.: National Museum of the American Indian, Smithsonian Institution, in association with National Geographic, 2004), 182; Patricia Pierce Erikson, "Decolonizing the "Nation's Attic: The National Museum of the American Indian and the Politics of Knowledge-Making in a National Space," in *The National Museum of the American Indian: Critical Conversation*, ed. Amy Lonetree and Amanda J. Cobb-Greetham (Lincoln: Univ. of Nebraska Press, 2008), 57–58.
7. William Raspberry, "This Museum Belongs on the Mall," Washington Post, June 5, 1987, A27.
8. H.R. 1570, 101st Congress (1989); H.R. 2477, 101st Congress (1989). Senator Simon introduced S.1959 on November 6, 1989, and his bill was very similar to the Lewis and Leland Bills, with one major exception: The Simon bill made clear that the museum's board of trustees had to operate subject to general policies established by the Smithsonian Board of Regents, and it gave the Regents, rather than the museum's board, the responsibility for operating the proposed affiliate program and national trust for African American museums. These

changes were undoubtedly in response to concerns raised by the Smithsonian.

9. "Smithsonian Institution Minority Employment Practices," *Hearings before the Government Activities and Transportation Subcomm. of the Comm. on Government Operations,* 101st Cong. 2 (1989).

10. Michael Welzenbach, "Lion of the Anacostia Museum," Washington Post, July 19, 1989, D10.

11. "Establishment of an African American Heritage Memorial Museum," *Hearing before the Subcomm. on Libraries and Memorials of the Comm. on House Administration,* 101st Cong. 34 (1989) (hereinafter "1989 House Hearing").

12. Kara Swisher, "Black History Museum Plan Sparks Debate," Washington Post, October 16, 1989, A1.

13. 1989 House Hearing, 42.

14. Kara Swisher, "Black History Museum Plan Sparks Debate," Washington Post, October 16, 1989, A1, A12.

15. 1989 House Hearing, 54–57. Thus, the objections expressed by Dr. Charles Wright, one of the founders of the AAMA, had been met by the efforts to build consensus since 1968. Gaither also entered into the record a survey commissioned by the AAMA, the "profile of Black museums," which was a comprehensive study of all of the local African American Museums published in 1988. John Fleming, the Director of the National Afro American Museum and Cultural Center in Wilberforce, submitted a statement requesting Federal assistance to the hearing, noting that the museum had been created with state and private funds. 1989 House Hearing, 121–124. But federal support for the Wilberforce Museum was still not forthcoming.

16. 1989 House Hearing, 35.

17. Ibid., 36.

18. Pub. L. No. 101-185, 103 Stat. 1336 (1989). The legislation directed the Smithsonian to construct at least 400,000 square feet of facilities on the National Mall, in New York City, and in Suitland, Maryland. The federal government was authorized to pay for 2/3 of the National Mall building, 1/3 of the New York building, and all of the Suitland building. Congress also established a trust fund to provide museum training to Indians so that its exhibits could travel to Indian museums and other facilities outside of Washington.

19. 1989 House Hearing, 32.

20. Judith Weinraub, "Smithsonian Launches Mall Project," Washington Post, December 12, 1989, D1.

21. Barbara Gamarekian, "National Black Museum Gains Support," Florida Today, June 24, 1990, 5F.

22. Jacqueline Trescott, "Toward a Black Museum," Washington Post, May 8, 1990, B2.

23. Final Report of the African American Institutional Study at 6 (1991).

24. Hearings on H.R. 5831, H.R. 5822 and H.R. 1246, *Before the Subcomm. on Public Buildings and Grounds of the H. Comm. on Public Works and Transportation,* 102nd Cong. 25–51 (1992).

25. Hearing on Smithsonian Institution, H.R.1246, National African American

Museum, Before the Subcomm. on Libraries and Memorials of Comm. on House Administration, 102nd Congress 8 (1992) (hereinafter "1992 House Hearing").

26. "Smithsonian Authorizes African American Museum," The Star-Democrat (Eston, Maryland), February 4, 1992, 8A.

27. African American Museum in Capitol Mall Okayed by Senate Panel," San Bernardino County Sun, June 18, 1992, A17.

28. 1992 House Hearing, 28–32.

29. Carl T. Rowan Jr., "A Black 'Presence' on the Mall is Not Enough," Washington Post, April 19, 1992, C8.

30. Ta-Nehisi Coates, "Case History: How the Effort to Build an African American Museum on the Mall Ended Up in a Black Hole," Washington City Paper, Feb. 6–12, 1998, 24–35, 34.

31. 1992 House Hearing, 56.

32. Ibid., 43.

33. Coates, Case history, 32.

34. 139 Cong. Rec. H4,166 (daily ed. June 28, 1993).

35. Eric Brace, "Senate Okays Museum Bill," Washington Post, October 5, 1992, C7.

36. See, e.g., "Oral History Interview with Jesse Helms, March 8, 1974," http://docsouth.unc.edu/sohp/A-0124/excerpts/excerpt_6780.html; Chuck Smith, "The Case Against Jesse Helms," Wall Street Journal, September 4, 2001, http://www.wsj.com/articles/SB122643894408618377.

37. "The King Holiday and Its Meaning: Remarks of Senator Jesse Helms," http://www.martinlutherking.org/helms.html, accessed July 30, 2016.

38. Robin Toner, "In North Carolina's Senate Race, A Divisive TV Fight Over 'Values'," New York Times, September 23, 1990, http://www.nytimes.com/1990/09/23/us/in-north-carolina-s-senate-race-a-divisive-tv-fight-over-values.html?pagewanted=all.

39. Fath Davis Ruffins, "Culture Wars Won and Lost," Radical History Review, Vol. 70, 78–101, 95–96 (Winter 1998); Jacqueline Trescott, "Museum Bill Dies in Senate," Washington Post, October 8, 1994, Page C1; Helen Dewar, "In Braun-Helms Fight, Senate Searched Soul," Washington Post, December 12, 2003, A8.

40. 140 Cong. Rec. S28,285, (daily ed. October 6, 1994).

41. 140 Cong. Rec. S28,877 (daily ed. October 7, 1994).

42. Mitchell Locin, "Plan for Black Museum Brings Out the Old Rebel in Jesse Helms," Chicago Tribune, July 10, 1994, C2.

43. Michael Kilian, "The Rise and Haul of the Smithsonian Empire," Chicago Tribune August 8, 1996, Page 1.

44. Natalie Hopkinson, "Separate But Equal Won't Work for Museums, Either," Palm Beach Post, February 22, 1998, 1E.

45. Coates, Case History, 26, 28.

46. Hopkinson, Palm Beach Post, February 22, 1998, 5E.

Chapter 7

1. Ta-Nehisi Coates, "Case History: How the Effort to Build an African-American Museum on the Mall Ended Up in a Black Hole," *Washington City Paper*, February 6–12, 1998, 26, 28.
2. Peter Slevin, "Black History Museum Has Artifacts but No Building," *Washington Post*, January 9, 2000, C9.

Chapter 8

1. Robert Wilkins, "How Much Longer Must We Wait?" *Washington Post*, August 5, 2001, B8.
2. National Museum of African American History and Culture Act of 2001, H.R. 1718, 107th Cong. (2001); *ibid.*, S. 829, 107th Cong. (2001).
3. Congressional Press Conference. May 3, 2001. http://www.c-span.org/video/?164059-1/africanamerican-history-museum. All quotes from the press conference were drawn from this source.
4. Lynne Duke, "Role of a Lifetime," *Washington Post*, August 19, 2007, D1, http://www.washingtonpost.com/wp-dyn/content/article/2007/08/18/AR2007081801113.html; "Frederick Douglass IV is not a Descendant of Frederick Douglass," Website of Frederick Douglass Family Initiatives, accessed August 7, 2016, http://www.fdfi.org/fake-fred.html.
5. National Museum of African American History and Culture Plan for Action Presidential Commission Act of 2001, Pub. L. No. 107–106, 115 Stat. 1009 (2001).

Chapter 9

1. Joint Resolution Honoring the Contribution of Blacks to American Independence, Pub. L. No. 98-245, 98 Stat. 111 (1984).
2. A rendering of the planned memorial can be found at Ed Dwight's website, accessed August 7, 2016, http://www.eddwight.com/memorial-public-art/black-revolutionary-war-patriots-memorial-constitution-gardens-washington-dc.
3. The sponsoring group revised its plans and won approval for a renewed effort, overseen by the National Mall Liberty Fund, to plan and construct a "commemorative work to slaves and free Black persons who served in the American Revolution" as soldiers, sailors, or civilians. President Obama signed this measure into law in 2013 and the group is moving forward with the project. Pub. L. No. 112-239 § 2860, 126 Stat. 2164 (2013). *See also* http://libertyfunddc.com/ (accessed July 23, 2016).
4. Robert L. Wilkins, "The Forgotten Museum," (unpublished manuscript, 2002).
5. National Museum of African American History and Culture Plan for Action Presidential Commission, "The Time Has Come," Report to the President and to the Congress (2003), 1, http://nmaahceis.si.edu/documents/The_Time_Has_Come.pdf.

Chapter 10

1. An Act Establishing a Commission of Fine Arts, Pub. L. No. 61-181, 36 Stat. 371 (1910) (codified at 40 U.S.C. §§ 9101–04 (2011)).

2. "Past Members of the Commission on Fine Arts," Commission on Fine Arts, accessed August 7, 2016, https://www.cfa.gov/history/past-commission-members.

3. "A History of the National Mall and Pennsylvania Avenue Historic Park," National Park Service, accessed July 24, 2016, https://www.nps.gov/nationalmall-plan/Documents/mallpaavhistory.pdf, at 2.

4. S. Rep. No. 57-166, at 28 (1902)("McMillan Plan").

5. "Arts and Industries Building," Smithsonian Institution Archives, accessed August 7, 2016, http://siarchives.si.edu/history/arts-and-industries-building.

6. Annual Report of the Board of Regents of the Smithsonian Institution, H.R. Doc. No. 55-309, pt. 2, at 10 (1898); Annual Report of the Board of Regents of the Smithsonian Institution, H.R. Doc. No. 57-707, pt. 2, at 16 (1901); Letter of Smithsonian Secretary S.P. Langley transmitting Plans for a New Building for the U.S. National Museum in H.R. Doc. No. 57-314, at 3 (1903).

7. McMillan Plan, 44.

8. An Act to Expedite the Construction of the World War II Memorial in the District of Columbia, Pub. L. No. 107-11, 115 Stat. 19 (2001).

9. National Museum of African American History and Culture Plan for Action Presidential Commission, Final Site Report (2003), 38, http://nmaahceis.si.edu/documents/Final_Site_Report.pdf (Hereinafter "Final Site Report").

10. Final Site Report, 39.

11. Final Site Report, 42.

12. Vietnam Veterans Memorial Visitor Center Authorization, Pub. L. No. 108–126, Title II, § 202, 117 Stat. 1349 (2003) (establishing the Reserve); An Act to establish within the Smithsonian Institution the National Museum of African American History and Culture, and for other purposes, Pub. L. No. 108-184, § 8(a)(3), 117 Stat. 2682 (2003) (exempting the NMAAHC from provisions of the Commemorative Works Act).

13. Final Site Report, 71.

14. 149 Cong. Rec. S7155 (daily ed. May 23, 2003).

15. 149 Cong. Rec. S8378-80 (daily ed. June 23, 2003).

16. *Hearing on H.R. 2205, Legislation to Establish Within the Smithsonian Institution a National Museum of African-American History and Culture, Before the Comm. on House Administration*, 108th Cong. 5 (2003).

17. Ibid., 40–43, 46–48.

18. Ibid., 60–72.

19. Letter from John V. Cogbill III, NCPC Chairman, to Congressman Bob Ney, Chairman of the Committee on House Administration, Nov. 6, 2003 (on file with the author); Letter from John V. Cogbill III, NCPC Chairman, to James Jukes of the Executive Office of the President, Nov. 24, 2003 (on file with the author).

20. 149 Cong. Rec. H11490 (daily ed. Nov. 18, 2003) (statement of Rep. Lewis).

21. 149 Cong. Rec. S15303-04 (daily ed. Nov. 20, 2013) (statement of Sen. Brownback).

22. Photo located at http://siarchives.si.edu/collections/siris_sic_12639, accessed July 24, 2016.

23. Letter from John V. Cogvill, III, NCPC Chairman, to Lawrence Small, Nov. 3, 2005 (on file with the author).

24. Remarks at a Celebration of National African American History Month, *Public Papers of the Presidents: George W. Bush*, 1:186–89 (2005).

Epilogue

1. "Smithsonian Digitization Office Digitizes 1 Millionth Object!", June 21, 2016, http://insider.si.edu/2016/06/smithsonian-digitizes-1-million-object-collections/;"National Museum of African American History and Culture Joins White House To Celebrate Black History Month," February 12, 2016, http://newsdesk.si.edu/releases/national-museum-african-american-history-and-culture-joins-white-house-celebrate-black-hist.

2. Interview with Dr. Richard Kurin, Smithsonian Acting Provost and Under Secretary for Museums and Research, July 21, 2016.

3. More information about some of the responsible individuals appears at the museum's website, accessed August 7, 2016, www.nmaahc.si.edu.

4. Jackie Mansky, "How One Woman Helped End Lunch Counter Segregation in the Nation's Capital," *Smithsonian Magazine*, June 8, 2016, http://www.smithsonianmag.com/history/how-one-woman-helped-end-lunch-counter-segregation-nations-capital-180959345/?no-ist; "Terrell Place/Hecht Company Site, African American Heritage Trail," Cultural Tourism DC, accessed August 7, 2016, https://www.culturaltourismdc.org/portal/terrell-place/-hecht-company-site-african-american-heritage-trail.

5. "Permanent Mary Church Terrell Exhibit Dedicated in Ceremony at Terrell Place in Downtown Washington, DC," Venable LLP, December 3, 2003, https://www.venable.com/NEP/pressreleases/NewsDetail.aspx?news=a6fa5b04-c8bd-4f9a-bbab-52b4493b0f25; Jean Efron, "Art Makes a Statement for Business, Too," *New York Times*, March 31, 2012, http://www.nytimes.com/2012/04/01/jobs/art-as-an-extension-of-the-corporate-image.html.

6. Remarks by the President at the Groundbreaking Ceremony of the National Museum of African American History and Culture, February 22, 2012, http://www.presidency.ucsb.edu/ws/index.php?pid=99597. Video of the groundbreaking is available from C-SPAN, https://www.c-span.org/video/?304542-1/african-american-national-museum-groundbreaking-ceremony.

7. Ibid.

8. Ibid.

9. Ibid.

10. U.S. Const. pbl.

11. Fact Sheet, "National Museum of African American History and Culture: Design and Construction," July 1, 2016, http://newsdesk.si.edu/factsheets/national-museum-african-american-history-and-culture-design-and-construction.

12. Fact Sheet, "National Museum of African American History and Culture," February 1, 2016, http://newsdesk.si.edu/factsheets/national-museum-african-american-history-and-culture.

INDEX

★